Cambridgeshire
MURDERS

Alison Bruce

Best Wishes

Alison Bruce

SUTTON PUBLISHING

First published in the United Kingdom in 2005 by
Sutton Publishing Limited · Phoenix Mill
Thrupp · Stroud · Gloucestershire · GL5 2BU

British Library Cataloguing in Publication Data
A catalogue record for this book is available from the British Library.

ISBN 0-7509-3914-1

For Jacen

Typeset in 10/13pt Sabon
Typesetting and origination by
Sutton Publishing Limited.
Printed and bound in England by
J.H. Haynes & Co. Ltd, Sparkford.

CONTENTS

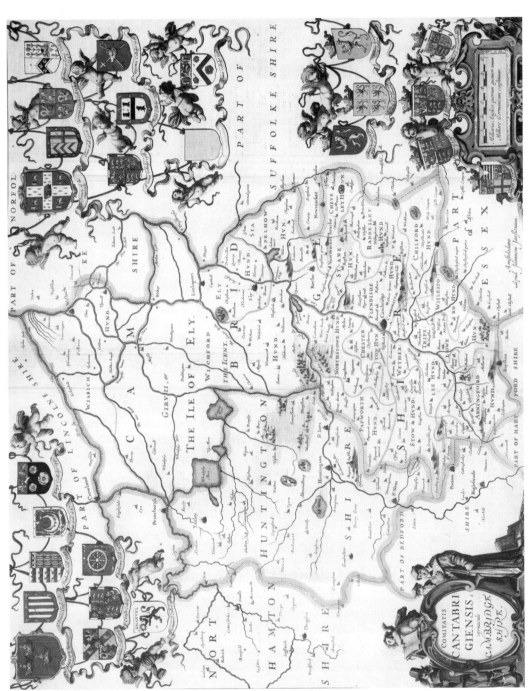

Map of Cambridgeshire and Huntingdonshire. (Cambridgeshire Collection, Cambridge Central Library)

INTRODUCTION

Cambridgeshire, which now incorporates its old neighbour Huntingdonshire, is largely rural and therefore not densely populated. Without any major cities, it is understandable that the crime rate for the county is lower than that of many other shires; but this does not mean that the murders that do occur there are in any sense mundane; in fact, many achieved such notoriety that they became cases of national interest.

When I first began to research this book I knew I would come across old and interesting murder cases that had not been fully documented. Those selected here cover three centuries of Cambridgeshire history, highlighting changes in society as well as trends in methods of committing murder. Although most cases were solved, in some the accuracy of the verdict and the fairness of the trial often served as good examples of why the laws allowing the admission of hearsay and circumstantial evidence needed to be changed; 'Arsenic and Old Laws' is a particularly good example.

Much of the research has involved going back to original assize and other period documents. Unfortunately, Cambridgeshire's inquest records relating to the period between the late 1800s and the late 1930s were destroyed by flooding – having been stored in a basement. Conversely, some of the best surviving documents are the oldest – the Ely Diocese Records include many sheets of beautiful handwritten statements, often signed by witnesses with a shaky 'X'.

While many of the county's murder cases are covered by the *Newgate Calendar*, I have not used this source verbatim: if you come across a copy you may notice differences between the details reported there and the information used in this book. This is because when cross-checking sources, I often found inaccuracies in the calendar – which of course does not mean that this is not an interesting source from which to initiate an investigation.

One reported murder that I chose not investigate further was the killing of a young lad named George Burnham. Although the case appears to be interesting, contemporary documentation was too limited to shed much more light on the case. The following is from the *Newgate Calendar* and demonstrates the sensationalist and 'fire and brimstone' nature of the publication:

RICHARD FAULKNER A Boy, executed at Wisbech, in 1810, for the Murder of another Lad of Twelve Years of Age
RICHARD FAULKNER was, at the Summer Assizes for Norfolk, 1810, capitally convicted of the wilful murder of George Burnham, a lad about twelve years of age, at Whittlesea, on the 15th of February, by cruelly beating him to death, for no other cause than for revenge on Burnham's mother, who had thrown some dirty water upon him.

The prisoner was not sixteen, but so shockingly depraved and hardened that after condemnation he repeatedly clenched his fist and threatened to murder the clergyman who attended the jail, or anyone who dared to approach him. Indeed he was so ferocious that the jailer found it necessary to chain his hands and feet to his dungeon, where he uttered the most horrid oaths and imprecations on all who came near him; and from the Friday to Saturday night refused to listen to any religious advice or admonition.

At length, to prevent the termination of his existence in this depraved state, the expedient was devised of procuring a child about the size of the one murdered, and similar in feature and dress, whom two clergymen unexpectedly led between them, by the hands, into the cell, where he lay sulkily chained to the ground; but on their approach he started, and seemed so completely terrified that he trembled in every limb; cold drops of sweat profusely fell from him, and he was almost continuously in such a dreadful state of agitation that he entreated the clergymen to continue with him, and from that instant became as contrite a penitent as he had before been callous and insensible.

In this happy transition he remained till his execution on Monday morning, having fully confessed his crime, and implored, by fervent prayer, the forgiveness of his sins from a merciful God!

Writing and researching this book has been a hugely enjoyable experience, especially when I have had the opportunity to see artefacts or visit places connected with the cases described. Walking along the narrow street outside Miss Lawn's old shop, seeing the hangman's noose that hanged one of these murderers or standing in a rainy Burwell churchyard next to the Flaming Heart were moments that made me feel as if I were touching Cambridgeshire's past. I hope that the cases included and the illustrations chosen will make some of the darkest stories from our county's history come alive for you too.

1
THE FLAMING HEART

One of England's earliest fairs was held at Stourbridge, Cambridge, and was granted a charter in 1211. Many authors wrote about the fair and in 1724 Daniel Defoe gave a detailed account: ' . . . it cannot be very unpleasant, especially to the trading part of the world, to say something of this fair, which is not only the greatest in the whole nation, but in the world . . .'.

The fair originally lasted for two days but by the middle of the sixteenth century it ran from 24 August to 29 September each year. A vast array of products was on sale until the last day, which was reserved as a horse-fair. Defoe's description notes:

> Towards the latter end of the fair, and when the great hurry of wholesale business begins to be over, the gentry come in from all parts of the county round; and though they come for their diversion, yet it is not a little money they lay out, which generally falls to the share of the retailers, such as toy-shops, goldsmiths, braziers, ironmongers, turners, milliners, mercers, etc., and some loose coins they reserve for the puppet shows, drolls, rope-dancers, and such like, of which there is no want, though not consider-able like the rest.

One of the puppet shows mentioned by Defoe belonged to Robert Shepheard, who was travelling towards Cambridge in the early part of September 1727 with his wife Martha, his daughter, also called Martha, and a couple of servants. Running low on funds, as they were passing through the village of Burwell they decided to raise some money by putting on a puppet show. On 8 September 1727 they hired a barn from a Mr Wosson. It was a clunch[1] barn with a thatched roof, and situated near Cockles Row.

The interior of the barn was approximately 17ft 6in high, 45ft long and 16ft 9in wide. The straw bales inside were stacked up to about 9ft, leaving about a third of the area available for the puppet show. Adjoining the building, and separated by just a lathe and plaster wall, was stabling. This partition was the same height as the stone walls of the barn, about 9ft, and the stable and its hayloft shared the same thatched roof as the barn.

The arrival of the puppet show caused much excitement in the village and there was a rush to gain admission at the price of 1*d* per person. With far more people wishing to see the show than the barn could hold, it was decided to lock the doors from the inside – many reports describe them as being 'nailed shut'.

The audience numbered in excess of a hundred with over half being made up of local children and families from nearby villages, including Reach,[2] Swaffham-Prior and Upware. Among them were villagers from all walks of life, including John and Ann Palmer, children of Henry and Sarah, who belonged to a prominent Burwell family, and Thomas Howe, his brother and sister Sarah.

At about nine in the evening a young ostler named Richard Whitaker was attending to Robert Shepheard's two horses in the adjacent stable. He was carrying a candle and a lantern. Wanting to see the puppet show but not wishing to pay the entrance fee, he climbed up into the hayloft where he was able to look down into the crowded barn. While there he threw hay down to the stable below; inevitably, some hay caught alight on the naked candle flame and Whitaker rushed from the building to raise the alarm.

In *An Account of a Most Terrible Fire* by Thomas Gibbons (see pages 3–4), young Thomas Howe described watching the show while sitting on a beam inside the barn. He was one of the first to spot the flames, which were 'so small that he thinks he could have enclosed it in his hands'. This small fire began high up in the building very close to the thatched roof, which was unusually dry due to a recent drought. As well as the straw and hay, the inside of the barn was draped in old cobwebs and the fire quickly took hold, rushing along the length of the thatch – according to the parish register, 'like lightning flew round the barn in an instant'.

A drawing of Burwell Barn in Cockles Row. (Cambridgeshire Collection, Cambridge Central Library)

The audience rushed to the door, which was not only sealed but also blocked by an oval table that the puppet master had used earlier in his show. In their desperation to escape they crowded the door and many ended up falling into a great heap behind it.

Outside the barn, the first to give assistance was a Wicken man, Thomas Dobedee, who happened to be in Burwell. Described as 'a very stout man, in the prime of life', he managed to force the door and began pulling survivors from the blaze.

Thomas Howe saw the doors open and leapt down from his beam on to the pile of bodies below, which he described as being three or four feet deep with not one person left standing. The parish register explains 'that most of those that did escape were forced to crawl over the heads and bodies of those that lay in a heap at the door'. Thomas Howe's brother clambered over the bodies accompanied by two smaller boys who refused to let go of him; all three

AN
ACCOUNT
OF A
Moſt Terrible FIRE

By THOMAS GIBBONS, D.D.

The title page of An Account of a Most Terrible Fire *by Thomas Gibbons, published in 1769.* (Floramay Waterhouse)

of them managed to reach safety. Two men who had escaped helped Dobedee to rescue others. Dobedee stayed so long that his hair was singed, having put his own life at tremendous risk.

The wind, however, remained strong, fanning the flames and sending burning stalks of straw into the air. Five other houses in the neighbourhood were razed to the ground, one of which was home to bed-ridden Mary Woodbridge, who perished.

After about half an hour the thatched roof collapsed and the last hope of rescuing anyone else vanished. Although Thomas Howe and his brother had survived, their sister had died, as had John and Ann Palmer. In total there were about eighty deaths, the bodies transported by cart and buried in two large pits in the graveyard. A gravestone known as 'The Flaming Heart' was erected in Burwell cemetery commemorating seventy-eight deaths, although a 1769 account lists seventy-nine with a possibility of two more unnamed victims. The bodies of John and Ann Palmer were buried separately since the Palmer family had its own dedicated area in the churchyard. A number of the casualties were children who had climbed from their bedroom windows to see the show. Also among the dead were the puppeteer and his family.

The sermon later preached by Alexander Edmondson, vicar of the parish, came from Lamentations 4: 8: 'Their visage is blacker than coal; they are not known in the streets; their skin cleaveth to their bones: it is withered, it is become like a stick.'

Richard Whitaker was arrested and charged with arson. He was about 25 years old and came from Hadstock in Essex. Some reports suggest that he was tried at the Essex Assizes, others that he was tried at the Cambridge Assizes. The original assize records for these hearings no longer exist but it seems most likely that he was tried in March 1728 in Cambridge.

Whitaker was found to have been the cause of the fire, but only through negligence, and so he was acquitted of the charge of arson. Parish records say 'that the fire was occasioned by the negligence of a servant who set a candle and lantern near the heap of straw which was in or near the barn'.

Apart from references to the fire in parish records the only other account of the day was a half-sheet produced by a Northampton printer very shortly afterwards. It contained several major inaccuracies including the date being wrong by a day and the listing of an incorrect number of casualties. However, it is still an interesting, if graphic, account:

September 9th, 1727. At Burwell in Cambridgeshire a Puppet Show was exhibited in a barn, ye doors were locked, and there was a stable adjoining to it where a boy was got with design to see it, for which purpose he climbed up upon some beams and took his candle with him, while he was viewing ye show fell down among a heap of straw and find it alight which ye boy perceiving he sprung out and narrowly escaped. The fire burning very fierce had catcht ye roof of this barn before ye people perceived it, ye doors were lockt to keep people out, and with some difficulty ye doors were broke and some escaped – but the rest pushing to get out wedged one another in yet none could stir till the roof fell in and 105 persons perished in ye flames. Some few were escapd into an adjoining yard which was built round with thatcht houses and on fire, but were forced to lie down and perish in it. An excise man and his child perished there and his wife is since quite distracted. After the fire was abated they found here an arm and there a leg, here a head there a body, some burnt with their bowels hanging out, most deplorable sight. There were abundance of people from the adjacent towns in ye number all most young persons.

The Revd Thomas Gibbons wrote *An Account of a Most Terrible Fire*, a more comprehensive account of the incident, published by J. Buckland in London in 1769. Gibbons had spent some of his childhood in Reach and in 1728 attended a school in Little Swaffham, just outside Burwell. He saw the site of the fire and many years later revisited Burwell and drew his account from village records and the memories of survivors, primarily Thomas Howe, who were keen to have the fire recorded more accurately than the account produced at the time.

The fire had a huge impact on the small rural village of Burwell and its surrounding hamlets. Of Burwell's 800 inhabitants at the time, it is said that barely a family escaped without loss.

The barn was located in Cockles Row, near the footpath which now runs between the pharmacy and the bank. Since the fire some villagers have claimed to have heard the ghostly clanking of water pails.

In February 1774 the following report appeared in the *Cambridge Chronicle*:

A report prevails that an old man died a few days ago at a village near Newmarket (Fordham), who just before his death seemed very unhappy;

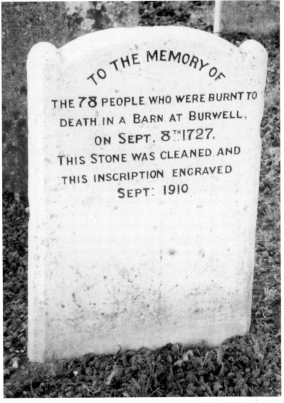

The back of the Flaming Heart, restored in 1910. (Jennifer Marrs)

said he had a Burthen on his Mind, which he must disclose. He then confessed that he set Fire to the Barn at Burwell on ye 8th. of September 1727, when no less than 80 persons unhappily lost their lives; that he was an Ostler at that Time, at or near Cambridge, and having an Antipathy to the Puppet Show Man was the cause of his committing that diabolical Action, which was attended with such dreadful consequences.

Frustratingly, the man is not named, therefore making it impossible to check the likelihood of this claim, but according to parish records the old man in question was not Richard Whitaker.

Notes

1 Clunch is a traditional building material, usually a soft limestone, often used in the east of England, where more durable stone is uncommon. It can be rich in iron-bearing clays or be very fine and white – in effect just chalk. As it is not a long-lasting material, it is now used mostly for boundary walls, and occasionally for traditional agricultural buildings. Clunch was quarried in Burwell.

2 Reach (sometimes spelt Reche) is the location of the Reach Fair, whose charter dates from 1201. The fair is still held in May each year, making it England's longest surviving fair.

2

ARSENIC
AND OLD LAWS

Amy Conquest[1] was born to Thomas and Mary Conquest in Whittlesey and baptised on 19 October 1729. The family were not well off but nevertheless Amy's parents ensured that she received an education until she reached the age of 12. By the age of 16 she had grown into a tall, fine girl and began to receive attention from Thomas Reed[2] of Whittlesey.[3] Her father did not approve of the liaison and wanted his daughter to stop seeing the young man, but the two had fallen in love and soon consummated their relationship, which, according to a later description in the *Newgate Calendar*, 'continued till it became criminal'.

Amy fully expected that she would marry and so was shocked when, in the summer of 1748, Thomas told her that he was planning to travel to London and did not know when he would come back to Whittlesey. Despite assuring her that they would marry upon his return, Amy still felt betrayed and began to spend time with another local man, John Hutchinson, who had also been a suitor but one she had not encouraged. Despite the fact that Amy had never particularly liked John, her family, and her father in particular, felt that he was a better choice than Thomas Reed. Consequently, when John formally asked for Amy's hand in marriage on 24 August 1748, her father was quick to consent. As the wedding was arranged for the very next day, Amy's father may have thought that a quick wedding would avoid any possibility of the union being spoilt by Thomas Reed's return.

However, Thomas got word that Amy and John Hutchinson were about to marry and rushed back to Whittlesey only to see the two leaving the church as man and wife. Amy was distraught when she saw him and instantly realised what a terrible mistake she had made by marrying a man she did not love.

Within days Thomas and Amy were seeing one another again but were not as discreet as they should have been. Very soon neighbours were gossiping and John Hutchinson became jealous. Amy's arguments with her husband culminated with him beating her with a belt or stick on several occasions, but also with a realisation that his wife would not change her ways. He began to drink heavily and to stay away from home.

At about 5 a.m. on 14 October, just seven weeks and one day after their wedding, John Hutchinson became ill, complaining of the 'ague'. Amy brewed him some warm ale but on seeing no improvement she sent for Mary Watson.

Mary stated that she found John very ill and that the boiled beer given to him by Amy had made him feel worse. According to some accounts John was still alive at 9 a.m., but died soon afterwards. Mary Watson claimed that:

> Ann Conquest, the sister of the said Amey [sister-in-law] went for this deponent in the afternoon following to desire after to come and see the said John and upon going he apprehended to this deponent to be dying and dyed within about three-quarters of an hour after. That he did not complain that any means had been used to shorted his life. That this deponent was at the laying out of the said John after death and that nothing appeared to her this deponent but that he dyed of his natural death.

Initially John's death was not considered suspicious, and the burial took place in Whittlesey on 16 October 1748. However, when Amy's lover moved in only a few days later in what seemed to be a blatant act of disrespect, the people of Whittlesey grew uneasy. On 19 October John's body was exhumed and three surgeons, John Clarke, William Benning and John Stona, carried out an autopsy. In the mid-eighteenth century methods of detecting and identifying poisons were primitive, so their account of their findings is both graphic and fascinating:

A statement from the inquest into the death of John Hutchinson. (Ely Diocese Records, Cambridge University Library)

We whose names are here unto subscribed being called upon the day and date above to open the body of John Hutchinson deceased found his stomach had been much inflamed and in it a bloody liquor with a mucus matter of the same colour which we imagine to be caused by some corrosive medicine taken inwardly.

The said liquor and mucus we immediately gave to a dog kept him confined and he expired about seven hours after.

The next day upon opening the dog found his stomach much in the same manner as the deceased John Hutchinson's and caused as we believe by the liquor out of his stomach.

The ensuing inquest heard statements from a variety of Whittlesey residents. One of the statements, which was to lead to Amy's arrest, came from shopkeeper William Hawkins, who testified that he had sold Amy Hutchinson an ounce of white arsenick[4] (sic) on Thursday 13 October. He said that she had wanted it to poison rats but could not say what use she had actually put it to.

By Tuesday 18 October Amy was under arrest and being held at the house of John Stona. A villager named Mary Addison, who asked her whether she had any poison in her house, visited her. Amy told her about the rat poison, saying that she had mixed it up with oatmeal and placed it under the floorboards. Mary went to the Hutchinson house the following morning where she found a broken pot containing the mixture Amy had described. Unfortunately for Amy, instead of retrieving it so that an attempt could be made to gauge the amount of arsenic it contained, Mary covered it with hay and left it there.

Most of the witness statements did not help Amy's situation. Even though Mary Watson said that John Hutchinson did not think he had been poisoned, telling the jury it was the beer that had made him worse would have weighed heavily against Amy. Even when John Hutchinson was portrayed at the inquest as a brutal man, the evidence did not lean in Amy's favour.

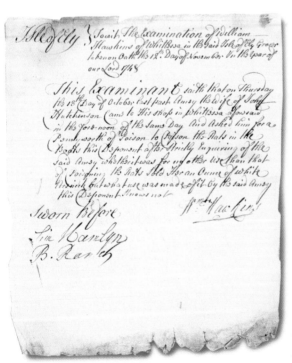

Another statement from the inquest. (Ely Diocese Records, Cambridge University Library)

An example of John Hutchinson's violence was relayed to the inquest jury by Prudence Watson of Whittlesey, who testified on 20 October. About three weeks earlier she had been at John and Amy's house. She and Amy had been drinking tea and decided to try reading their tea leaves when John returned home. After an angry exchange with his wife, John turned on Prudence and kicked her down the stairs. Prudence explained to the inquest that soon after this assault she had received a visit from Amy, who suggested that, as she was pregnant, she should

Prudence Watson's statement

press charges. Amy also stated that she feared that her husband 'would knock her on the head'. However, instead of winning any sympathy for Amy, Prudence's disclosure was seen as a sign of Amy's faithlessness and willingness to betray her husband.

Many of the statements were little more than hearsay and gossip, including accounts of tea-leaf reading from Alice Hardley (the mother of Amy's sister-in-law Ann) who said that Amy had seen a man's coffin and a child's coffin in her cup. There was a questionable statement from Alice Oldfield, who claimed that Prudence Watson had talked about an unnamed man who had died and whose wife was under suspicion; Alice suspected this to be Amy.

Statements such as this offered little in the way of evidence but they do show the weight given to rumour. It is possible that many of the friends, neighbours and even relatives who gave evidence against Amy at the inquest and the trial did not distinguish between scandal-mongering among themselves and testifying under oath. Unfortunately for Amy, when the inquest jury returned its verdict on Monday 7 November, the opening words demonstrated the damage that had been done:

Alice Oldfield's statement.
(Ely Diocese Records, Cambridge University Library)

the said John Hutchinson was wilfully and maliciously murdered by poison of which the said John on Fryday the fourteenth day of October last languished and dyed that it does not appear to them who were the person or persons that committed the said murder but that they have just reason to suspect that the same was committed and done by Amey the wife of the said John.

On 12 November summons were issued for witnesses to appear at the next Ely Assize or General Gaol Delivery. Records exist showing that among those to receive a summons were John Hammant, John Clark, John Stona, William Benning, William Hawk, Thomas Boon, Ann Baggerley and Alice Setchells, and that failure to appear in court 'and there give such evidence as one knoweth against Amey Hutchinson' would result in a £20 fine being issued upon the individual and their heirs. Of course £20 would have been a vast sum of money and these witnesses would have taken their duty very seriously.

Prudence Watson elaborated on her previous statement and claimed that Amy did not care about her husband, would like to 'get shot of him' and 'that she didst not go to bed without taking a knife along with her'. Prudence also named Thomas Reed, butcher, as a regular visitor to Amy's house, although she only said that he had attempted to get in and made no mention of reports that he had moved in after John Hutchinson's death. Strangely, Thomas Reed was not called to give evidence.

Nor do there appear to be any surviving copies of Amy's own statements or the numerous appeals that were said to have taken place.

Amy was arrested and charged with petit (petty) treason, which was essentially the same as murder, but was considered to be more serious because the murderer was in a position of trust in relation to the victim. Petit treason applied to the murder by a woman of her husband or a servant of his master or a clergyman of his superior: in all these cases the victims were considered to be the killer's superiors in law. In the 1750s William Blackstone wrote the following in his *Commentaries on the Laws of England*: 'The punishment of petit treason in a man was to be drawn and hanged, and in a woman to be drawn and burnt' and later in the same publication that this 'was the usual punishment for all sorts of treasons committed by those of the female sex'.

Burning at the stake was abolished in 1790. From 1700 until this date women who were sentenced to be burned were strangled with a rope first. However, in several instances this was attempted only as the fire was kindling, the result being that the fire often started burning the unfortunate condemned before the executioner could strangle her. The last time a woman had been burnt at the stake in Ely was when Mary Bird had been executed for petit treason on 1 July 1737.

The final surviving document on the Amy Hutchinson case from the Ely Diocese Records is dated 10 October 1949, almost a year later than the other statements; it is the verdict from a trial said to have lasted for four hours at which Amy always protested her innocence. It concludes:

The said John Hutchinson not in the least suspecting any poison to have been mixed or compounded with the said potion but believing the said potion to be wholesome . . . by which taking and swallowing the said potion so as aforesaid compounded mixed vitiated and infected with the said poison called Arsenick the said John Hutchinson then and there became sick and greatly distempered in his body of which sickness and distemper the said John Hutchinson from the aforesaid fourteenth day of October in the year aforesaid until the fifteenth day of the same month of October did languish and languishing did live on which said fifteenth day of October died.

And so the jurors upon their oaths do say that the said Amey Hutchinson the said John Hutchinson her late husband in manner and form aforesaid feloniously, traitorously, wilfully and of her malice aforethought did poison kill and murder against the law of our said Lord the King his Crown and Dignity.

Ely Assizes were held only once each year, and while awaiting trial Amy was held in the Ely Gaol (now Ely Museum). The assizes were regarded as a great social event and attracted large crowds. Many assize towns in the shire counties had designated 'hanging days', often market days to ensure the biggest crowd: the spectacle of the execution was intended to deter as many as possible from committing crimes.

The 1749 Assizes were a particular attraction because two people, Amy Hutchinson and John Vicars, were being tried for murder, and, as leniency in murder cases was rare, spectators had a good chance of seeing an execution. Curiously, both John Vicars and Amy Hutchinson were from Whittlesey and were on trial for the murder of their spouses. Amy had been married for just seven weeks and Vicars for about ten. But there the similarities ended, as after weeks of

The former Ely Gaol, now Ely Museum. (Cambridgeshire Collection, Cambridge Central Library)

bad relations with his new wife, John Vicars had openly gone to the shop where she worked and cut her throat, then ran into the street and shouted for someone to arrest him. It was said that he admitted that 'he dearly loved his wife, but her provocation was so great, and she was such a damned whore that he could not let her live, nor live without her'. The verdict at his trial declared that he:

> Feloniously wilfully and of his malice aforethought did make an assault and that he the said John Juckers, otherwise Vicars, with a certain knife of the value of four pound which he the said John Juckers, otherwise Vicars, then and there had and hold the said Mary Juckers, otherwise Vicars, in and upon the left side of the neck or throat ... one mortal wound of the breadth of three inches and of the depth of four inches of which said mortal wound the said Mary Juckers, otherwise Vicars, from the said twenty-fifth day of April in the year aforesaid until the twenty-seventh day of the same month of April ... of the said mortal wound died.

Vicars readily admitted his guilt at the assizes, his only request being that he wished to see Amy Hutchinson dispatched first. This was an unusual request in that it was common for the burning of women to occur after the other condemned prisoners had been hanged; but the wish was granted. Both were executed on 7 November 1749. A sledge drew Amy Hutchinson to the execution site and 'her face and hands being smeared with tar, and having a garment dawb'd with pitch, after a short prayer, the executioner strangled her, and 20 minutes after, the fire was kindled, and burnt half an hour'. Despite the spectacle of the execution, there was some disquiet in the crowd, since there had been no solid evidence against Amy and she had never admitted her guilt.

One week after Amy's death at least two publications carried her 'confessions': the *Norwich Mercury* of 9 November 1749 contained a full account, purportedly in Amy's own words. Then the November 1749 edition of the *Gentleman's Magazine* repeated most of the account in the form of a letter from an unnamed third person who had recounted the story 'chiefly' from Amy's own words.

The origin of both is a document witnessed by the gaoler Mr Alday. Amy only 'signed' with a cross, and yet she had received schooling until the age of 12 so should have been able to write her name. By contrast, the words of the statement appear to have been written by someone who had received a better education than Amy.

Whether or not the confession is genuine will never be known, but it remains an interesting and enlightening document. The final sentences are typical of the reported last words of condemned prisoners; they warn the public against bad conduct and perhaps do not ring as true as the earlier reference to another prisoner she calls T.N. If the entire statement was a fabrication it seems illogical that this passage was included as it not only shows the gaol in a bad light but also elicits some sympathy for Amy.

A drawing purportedly showing Amy Hutchinson's execution, but Amy was actually dead before the fire was started. (Cambridgeshire Collection, Cambridge Central Library)

The *Norwich Mercury* reported:

The following is the NARRATIVE of the life of Amy Hutchinson as taken from her own mouth:

I was born of honest and industrious parents, and my Mother still living, of whom, next to God, I ought in duty to beg forgiveness, having by the scandal of my life reflected disgrace upon her, but very undeservedly; for I was put to school and taught to read, and brought up in a sober, regular family, 'till about 12 years of age: At which time I was taken notice of by one T.R. and much in his favour; who when I grew up to 15 or 16 made his addresses to me in the way of courtship, but without my parents consent, my own father being then alive, who being acquainted by neighbours of the correspondence carried on between us, which had ripen'd into a detestable sin, absolutely forbad the continuance of it, warned T.R. not to come to the house, and wholly debarred me from him.

Apprehensive of what might follow, tho' he had promised me marriage, T.R. now pretended a great desire of seeing London first and I growing as suspicious that this might be an expedient to leave me in my shame, was as earnest to divert him from the journey, but finding I could not prevail, we parted in great wrath; and John Hutchinson coming in that evening (who likewise courted me, but to whom I had given no encouragement before) I consented to marry him the next day. I had heard that T.R. was set out on his journey to London, however he was not gone so far but a messenger overtook him, and he was at the church door when our wedding was just over.

In three or four days after I was married, my former suitor renewed his application with threatnings, that my husband and I should not live long together; and again said, *That if I did not kill my husband, he would kill me*, and advised me to poison him; and about ten or eleven o'clock one night; when I had not been married a week, my husband being abroad, T.R. having a hanger, thrust it thro' the Window, and said, *He would stab me if I did not follow his advice*; being interrupted by some neighbours going by, he went away, but never left teasing me till I promised him to undertake that abominable act, for which I now abhor myself and repent in dust and ashes.

My late husband John Hutchinson was an Irishman, and had lived about a year and half in the town, supporting himself decently by his honest labour. His addresses to me were private, but without any indecent liberties; and when I over night consented to have him, he joyfully accepted my declaration in his favour; and procuring a licence next morning we were married; and to the time of his unhappy death, lived together about ten weeks. I must do him the justice to say, that if my behaviour had been dutiful and faithful to him, I might have lived very happily with him.

My mother and father-in-law were well reconciled to us, and every thing spoke peace and quiet, till T.R. came to me, and my husband was by my own mother and others acquainted with his frequent and public visits to me. From this discovery he grew disturbed, uneasy and peevish, and several times beat me with a belt or a stick; and tho' he never reproached me with the cause of his anger, told me I knew what it was for, and I verily believed if I could have refrained from the company of T.R. my husband would have left off his correction, which I justly deserved; and if effectual, would have prevented a sorer punishment. However, as my heart was never wholly his, and this ill treatment (as I thought it) urged me on, so it was unhappy on his part, that he seeing no amendment in me, fell into company, and took to spending his time and money abroad, and by that means left me too unguarded to the wiles of my seducer, to whom I once more abandon'd myself, forgetting all reputation, reason and humanity.

By his wicked advice I bought poison, and was directed how to use it, and to give it my husband in some warm ale, accordingly I bought some poison of Mr. Hawkins on the Thursday, and my husband happened to have two or three fits of an ague, this seemed a fit occasion to give him the fatal draught, which I did about five o'clock on the Friday morning, and about nine the same morning, going over the market place (for my mother coming in had sent me for a little wine for my husband) I told T.R. what I had done, and that my husband was yet alive, and he bid me get some more poison, as I did then of Mr. Gibbs, but there was no need of it, for my husband died the Friday about one o'clock. My mother finding that day the poison I bought last, first taxed me with a suspicion, and said, *I am afraid you have done something to your husband*, and I answered, *What makes you think so mother*, but she never gave me the reason.

My husband was buried on the Sunday evening, T.R. having never come near me for three days past, which was a longer time than he usually intermist'd his visits, came next Monday morning, and renewed his courtship, having all the time promised me marriage if my husband was dead. About noon of that day I was seized on suspicion, and my late husband's body being taken up, the coroner's inquest sat upon it, and declared he died of poison; and upon my trial at Ely, which lasted upwards of four hours and where I had the assistance of counsel as far as my case would admit, I was justly convicted of being the guilty person who administered it.

As it is the fate of wretches given over to their wickedness, to fall from one step to another, so it was my case: for being quite forsaken by T.R. who never visited me since the day I was first in custody; and being conscious that such a sentence as I deserved might pass upon me, I was partly drawn by the insinuations of one T.N. a fellow prisoner, pretending it would be a means to get me off at the assizes,[5] and partly by force, to a lewd action which I ought to have complained of as a rape; for he stopped my mouth with my apron, that I could not cry out, and it was so far my fault, that I did not make my complaint till a fortnight after; when I told the gaoler.

There are many other reports raised of a chicken poison'd, and of lewdness with other persons, which I do solemnly declare to be false. I have here truly confessed the heavy burden of my sins which has sore oppressed my mind, and hope God of his mercy will relieve that weight, and restore me, most unworthy as I am, to his grace and favour for Christ Jesus sake, who came into the World to save sinners, of whom I acknowledge myself one of the greatest.

All the Good I can now do, after my repentance and prayer to God (in which I have the assistance of Christ's Ministers) is, First, To warn all young persons to acquaint their friends when any Addresses are made to them; and above all, if any base or lewd persons dare to assault you with anything shocking to modest and chaste ears.

Second, That they should never leave a person they are engaged to in a pet, nor wed another to whom they are indifferent in spite; for if they come together without affection, the smallest matter will separate them.

Third, That being married, all persons should mutually love, forgive and forbear, and leave no room for busy meddlers to raise and foment jealousy between two who should be one. And Fourth. If after all diabolical temper

The door removed from Ely Gaol in 1820. (Stewart P. Evans)

should adventure to do that, it becomes the duty of an honest woman to reveal the first instance of such attempts, to her husband or relation; and guard herself by all the powers of grace, and assistance of good friends, to prevent the ill effects, and to rely upon the protection of good Providence in these best endeavours, that he will either remove the temptation, or make way to escape it.

Sign'd, A. H. Amy Hutchinson, her mark.

In the presence of Mr Alday, Gaoler, &c.

It is only thanks to one of the remaining statements that we know Amy Hutchinson's lover as Thomas Reed rather than just T.R. Unfortunately, the information held in parish records at this time was sparse and often incomplete – it was only in the 1830s that the requirement to include a parishioner's occupation was introduced – so the references to Thomas Reed in the Whittlesey parish records may refer to more than one person (although they never overlap and only one Thomas Reed was christened and buried in the parish at the time). Listed here are all the entries relating to Thomas Reed, or Read as his name was also spelt.

10th February 1725	Thomas Read, son of George and Ann christened.
30th April 1749	Thomas Read married Mary Sudbury,
8th May 1750	Isabel, daughter of Thomas and Mary christened.
18th November 1751	Thomas, son of Thomas and Mary christened.
20th November 1751	Thomas, son of Thomas and Mary buried.

28th September 1752   Anne Read, buried.
21st October 1753   Robert, son of Thomas and Anne christened.
25th November 1753   Robert Read, buried.
1st September 1767   Thomas Read buried.
1st May 1769   Jane Read, widow of Thomas buried.

If all the entries do belong to Amy's Thomas then he was hardly heartbroken, having married for the first time less than six months before her execution and in total marrying three times, outliving two wives and at least three of his four children. At the very least he should have been called as a witness at both the inquest and her trial. If her confession were true then he played an active part in John Hutchinson's murder and should have been tried alongside her. His relationship with Amy was without doubt a catalyst for the killing, and whether he was involved or not it is clear that he could have been executed too, and surely had a lucky escape.

Notes

1 According to parish records her name was spelt 'Amy' at her christening, but is then spelt 'Amey' on her marriage certificate and in the assize records. Unless quoting from original documents the spelling 'Amy' has been used.
2 Spelt 'Reed' in the one surviving assize record but all residents of Whittlesey at the time with that name spelt it 'Read'.
3 Variously spelt 'Whitlesea', 'Whittlesea' and 'Whittlesey'. Unless quoting from original documents the current spelling 'Whittlesey' has been used.
4 Arsenic is a metallic element, traces of which are found in all human tissue. Historically it was an easy choice for poisoners as it was readily available, especially as a pesticide or rat poison. Acute arsenic poisoning affects the digestive system and symptoms can appear within thirty minutes, the most notable being gastric fever, often accompanied by sickness and bloody diarrhoea. With severe poisoning death can occur in as little as a few hours.
5 This may have been an attempt by Amy to get pregnant, as it was then illegal to execute a pregnant woman. If condemned, a pregnant woman would be allowed to give birth before being executed; the child would normally have been farmed out to a wet nurse, and in many cases would have died soon afterwards.

3
PRIME MINISTER'S ELIMINATION TIME

In the unique case of an English Prime Minister being assassinated, Cambridgeshire can claim two connections: the victim, Spencer Perceval, although born in London on 1 November 1762, completed his education at Trinity College, Cambridge, before becoming Prime Minister on 4 October 1809. His killer, John Bellingham, was a Cambridge man by birth, having been born in North Street, St Neots, in around 1771.

While still a teenager Bellingham began a successful business in marine products. In 1800 he visited Archangel in Russia, returning to England in 1802. The following year he married Mary Neville, and in 1804 made another visit to Archangel. But then things began to go wrong for him. The ship in which his cargo was held – referred to variously as the *Soyuz* or *Sojus* – sank in the White Sea. Suspecting fraud, Lloyds of London refused to pay against the insurance. They had been alerted by an anonymous letter, which the ship's owners, Van Brienen, suspected had been sent by Bellingham himself. This prompted Soloman Van Brienen to begin legal proceedings against Bellingham, accusing him of debt.

Far left: *A contemporary engraving of Spencer Perceval.* (Source unknown) Left: *John Bellingham, as depicted during his trial.* (W. Medland)

Bellingham managed to reach the British Ambassador, but his request for help was denied and he was arrested. He subsequently spent two years in gaol, during which time his business fell into debt. When the initial charges against him were dropped his incarceration continued on the grounds of bankruptcy. In total, Bellingham was in prison for almost six years.

Released in 1808, by the following year he had found his way back to England. With feelings of bitterness at his abandonment by the British government, he wrote many letters attempting to claim compensation for his ordeal. One reply came from Spencer Perceval's office, informing him that his claim was baseless.

During February 1812 he took lodgings in New Millman Street, London, and in March sent the following letter to the police magistrates of Bow Street:

TO THEIR WORSHIPS THE POLICE MAGISTRATES
OF THE PUBLIC OFFICE IN BOW STREET
Sirs,

I much regret its being my lot to have to apply to your worships under most peculiar and novel circumstances. For the particulars of the case I refer to the enclosed letter of Mr. Secretary Ryder, the notification from Mr. Perceval, and my petition to Parliament, together with the printed papers herewith. The affair requires no further remark than that I consider his Majesty's Government to have completely endeavored to close the door of justice, in declining to have, or even to permit, my grievances to be brought before Parliament for redress, which privilege is the birthright of every individual. The purport of the present is, therefore, once more to solicit his Majesty's Ministers, through your medium, to let what is right and proper be done in my instance, which is all I require. Should this reasonable request be finally denied, I shall then feel justified in executing justice myself – in which case I shall be ready to argue the merits of so reluctant a measure with his Majesty's Attorney-General, wherever and whenever I may be called upon so to do. In the hopes of averting so abhorrent but compulsive an alternative I have the honour to be, sirs, your very humble and obedient servant,

JOHN BELLINGHAM
No. 9 NEW MILLMAN STREET,
March 23, 1812

This letter was communicated to Members of Parliament, but no action was taken. Having again applied to the Treasury for assistance, to no avail, Bellingham decided that revenge was his only option and methodically set about becoming acquainted with the House and its members. He bought a pair of pistols and ammunition and became a frequent visitor to parliament. On 20 April he visited a tailor and asked him to alter his overcoat to accommodate a 9in inside breast pocket.

At 5.15 p.m. on 11 May 1812 Prime Minister Perceval and some aides entered the lobby entrance to the House of Commons. Bellingham had been sitting by the fire waiting: he crossed towards Perceval and pulled a pistol from his coat pocket, fired a single round into the Prime Minister and calmly returned to his seat.

One of Perceval's companions, Lord Osborne, rushed forward to catch the Prime Minister, and with assistance from the other ministers carried him into the Speaker's Rooms. It was immediately obvious however that nothing could be done.

The exits were closed and someone shouted out 'Where's the murderer?', to which Bellingham replied, 'I am the unfortunate man'.

Asked why he had shot Perceval, Bellingham replied, 'Want of redress, and denial of justice'. One of the witnesses to the shooting, the solicitor Henry Burgess, approached Bellingham and asked, 'You have another pistol?' Bellingham replied in the affirmative. 'Is it loaded?' Burgess asked. Again Bellingham replied 'Yes.' Burgess searched Bellingham and retrieved a second small pistol.

At about 5.30 p.m. Dr William Lynn arrived from Great George Street, Westminster. He stated that:

> His [Perceval's] body was partly off the table; his shirt and white waistcoat were bloody; and on examining the body, I found a wound of the skin about over the fourth rib on the left side near the breastbone. The wound had the appearance of a large pistol ball having entered. On examining his pulse, I found he was quite dead. I then passed a probe to ascertain the direction of the ball, and found it had passed obliquely downwards and inwards in the direction of the heart. The wound was at least 3 in deep, and I have no doubt that it caused his death.

A contemporary illustration depicting the assassination of Spencer Perceval. (St Neots Museum)

Bellingham was taken to Newgate Prison and at 10 a.m. on Tuesday 12 May an inquest was opened in the Rose & Crown public house. On the same day Bellingham sent the following letter to his landlady:

Dear Madam,

Yesterday midnight I was escorted to this neighbourhood by a noble troop of Light Horse, and delivered into the care of Mr. Newman (by Mr. Taylor the Magistrate and MP) as a state prisoner of the first class. For eight years I have never found my mind so tranquil as since this melancholy but necessary catastrophe, as the merits or demerits of my peculiar case must be regularly unfolded in a criminal court of justice, to ascertain the guilty party, by a jury of my country.

I have to request the favour of you to send me three or four shirts, some cravats, handkerchiefs, night-caps, stockings, etc, out of my drawers, together with comb, soap, toothbrush, with any other trifle which presents itself which you may think I may have occasion for, and enclose them in my leather trunk, and the key, please to send sealed per bearer; also my great-coat, flannel gown, and black waistcoat, which will much oblige.

Dear madam, your obedient servant, John Bellingham.

To the above please to add the Prayer Book.

On Friday 15 May Bellingham appeared at the Old Bailey before the Lord Mayor and the judges, Lord Chief Justice Mansfield, Baron Graham and Sir Nash Grose. He was refused the option of putting in a plea of insanity and instead pleaded 'not guilty'.

At the trial, despite the several lengthy statements he made in his defence, he was found guilty. Until the time of his execution he was allowed only bread and water, and all means by which he may have been able to attempt suicide were eliminated. What most distressed him, however, was being unable to shave and so appearing ungentlemanly.

The execution took place at Newgate on 18 May, at 8 a.m. An hour later his body was transported to the morgue of St Bartholomew's Hospital, where he was dissected 'in the furtherance of medical science'. He left behind three sons; Spencer Perceval twelve children.

Bellingham left the following letter for his wife:

MY BLESSED MARY

It rejoiced me beyond measure to hear you are likely to be well provided for. I am sure the public at large will participate in, and mitigate, your sorrows; I assure you, my love, my sincerest endeavours have ever been directed to your welfare. As we shall not meet any more in this world, I sincerely hope we shall do so in the world to come. My blessing to the boys, with kind remembrance to Miss Stephens, for whom I have the greatest regard, in consequence of her uniform affection for them. With the purest

John Bellingham, sketched while in the morgue. (Norris Museum, St Ives)

intentions, it has always been my misfortune to be thwarted, misrepresented and ill-used in life; but however, we feel a happy prospect of compensation in a speedy translation to life eternal. It's not possible to be more calm or placid than I feel, and nine hours more will waft me to those happy shores where bliss is without alloy.

Yours ever affectionate,
JOHN BELLINGHAM.

The assassination of Spencer Perceval was surrounded by some quirky stories. On 11 May Perceval told his wife that he had dreamt a man in the House of Commons had shot him. John Williams, a wealthy mining engineer, dreamt of the exact details of the assassination. This vision came to him after the event but well before the news could have reached him in Cornwall. At the other end of the country, in a village near Gretna Green, the news of the assassination was passed to the *Dumfries and Galloway Courier* on 10 May, before the assassination had taken place. In the General Election of 1983 one of Bellingham's descendants, Henry Bellingham, was elected as Conservative Member for Norfolk North West constituency; in 1997 one of his opponents was Roger Percival, by coincidence a descendant of Spencer Perceval.

Perceval was not well liked and when the news of his death reached many parts of the country it was greeted with great celebration.

4

THE EARLY BIRD CATCHES THE KILLER

Some people quite literally get away with murder, but because of a coincidental meeting with a sharp-witted woman, this was not to be the case for Thomas Weems of Godmanchester.

Thomas was a strongly built man in his early twenties when, around the start of 1818, he began courting a local girl, Mary Ann Sawyer. Mary was still in her teens and described as being of a 'very unprepossessing appearance'. Before long their relationship faltered, and so, in order to hold on to her lover, Mary claimed that she was pregnant. Thomas did his best to disentangle himself, even moving from Godmanchester to Great Staunton, where he was eventually arrested and forced to accept responsibility for Mary and their unborn child.

Thomas found work in a mill near Goldington, Bedfordshire, and although the couple married at the local church, they did not live together; Thomas chose to live in Goldington while Mary returned to Godmanchester to live with her grandfather in St Ann's Lane. When, during Thomas's several visits to Mary over the following months, it became apparent that Mary had lied and the pregnancy was false, Thomas left his job and searched for other work, moving south until he eventually took employment as a miller in Edmonton, north London.

He had only been in Edmonton for a short time when he met Maria Woodward, whom he described as 'as fine a young woman as any in the world'. After a courtship of about two months he proposed and she accepted. It seems that it was at this point that he decided that he would have to murder his wife. He told Maria that he needed to return to Huntingdon for money, and that they would marry as soon as he returned.

At the start of May Thomas began his journey back to Godmanchester. On the way he met John Beck, a postboy. The two had grown up together in Godmanchester, and Beck, returning to Huntingdon from Royston, offered him a lift in his chaise.[1] It seems that it never occurred to Thomas Weems that he should have been more discreet. On their journey Thomas told John of his new position in Edmonton and that he had met a young woman whom he was determined to marry. John was aware that Thomas was already married and warned him against bigamy. Thomas replied to this was that he was going to fetch his wife and would soon get rid of her.

John dropped Thomas on the outskirts of Godmanchester, but saw Thomas and Mary together later in the week, early on Thursday evening. Thomas informed him that they would be leaving for Edmonton the following morning while his wife said that they were planning to walk. John was shocked and told Thomas that it would be impossible for Mary to walk that far. The reply was that, if that was the case, she 'might stop on the road and be damned'.

Thomas and Mary left early on the morning of Friday 7 May[2] and after about 15 or 16 miles of constant walking they stopped near the villages of Wendy and Arrington and Mary lay down on the grass to rest.

Susannah Bird lived in Wendy and had set out to travel to Royston. Ahead of her she saw a man and woman sitting at the roadside; the woman sat on the right-hand side of the road near a field belonging to a local farmer called Mr Russell, and the man sat opposite and was toting a bundle. Susannah passed by, but after she had walked on a little further she looked back and saw that they had both entered Mr Russell's field. They stood looking around them and she thought they might be watching her. She looked back several times but eventually lost sight of them and walked on to Royston.

It was about one o'clock when Susannah made her return journey. On meeting Thomas, who was still carrying the bundle but continuing his journey alone, she asked what had become of the woman he had been with. 'I left her behind', he replied. 'She is about spun up. I cannot get her any further, so I left her to get on by the coach.'

Unfortunately for him, Susannah Bird was not the sort of woman who took things at face value, and while he walked on she looked out for the coach. When it arrived she looked both inside and out but did not spot Mary. This raised her suspicions further. She saw a Mr Sell hoeing in the field next to Mr Russell's and told him of her concerns, saying she 'would go to the next field, and see if she could discover what betided the young woman'.

On doing so Susannah immediately discovered that the grass was trodden down 'as if some persons had been struggling on the ground' and then spotted a finger and a pair of shoes protruding from a pile of grass. She called out to Mr Sell, who quickly uncovered a body. Mary Ann Weems was lying in a ditch, her face obscured by her shawl and bonnet. There was also the mark of a man's footprint in the ground. Susannah described the body later, in court: 'the face and neck were very black, appeared to have been caused by strangulation, as there was a coloured garter round the neck, with a slip noose drawn very tight.'

Travelling along the same road was the Revd Mr Brown, a magistrate from Conington who drew level with the field just as the body was being uncovered. Susannah gave him an accurate description of Thomas. Brown issued an arrest warrant and dispatched the local constable, Jackson, along with an assistant. The men took a chaise and followed the fugitive south, apprehending him as he rode in a wagon between Puckeridge and High Cross.

The county coroner opened the inquest at 8 p.m. and had barely finished swearing in the jury when the magistrate and constables arrived with Thomas in custody. The inquest continued into the night, eventually closing after 1 a.m. on Saturday 8 May. The jury returned a verdict of wilful murder against Thomas Weems, who was immediately taken to the county gaol at Cambridge to await trial at the next assizes.

On Wednesday 4 August 1819 Thomas was brought before Mr Justice Burrough. John Beck, Susannah Bird and the inhabitants of Wendy who had been involved in the discovery of Mary's body and the felon's apprehension were all called as witnesses. Maria Woodward came from Edmonton to give evidence. She described how she had met Thomas Weems after he had taken up his position at the mill. He had told her he was a single man, and they had courted for nine weeks before his proposal, which she had immediately accepted. She gave her evidence but was clearly upset. At her distress Thomas reached out and they shook hands.

The other witness of note was Mr Orridge, the Cambridge gaoler, who said that he had been present on two occasions when Thomas had received visitors. One was his father and the other his sister. It was during his sister's visit that Orridge had overheard Thomas say that it 'was no use denying it any longer, as he should be telling a falsehood every time, which would be only adding one sin to another'. Shortly after this, he had confessed and his confession was read out to the court:

> After I had been at work at Randall's, of Edmonton, about a month, I formed an acquaintance with Maria Woodward, whom I told that I was single, and promised her marriage, and then made up my mind to return into Huntingdonshire to murder my wife. I thought of cutting her throat, but afterwards changed my mind; and if I could hang her I would. On the 1st of May I left Edmonton for Godmanchester, and on the 5th returned for Edmonton about 5 o'clock in the morning. After proceeding on the journey 14 or 15 miles, my wife complained of being tired. I asked her whether she had not some toast in her pocket that was left at breakfast, she said yes; I then said, you can sit down and eat it, and I will take a nap until the coach comes up. We sat down together, and she began to eat; at this moment the horrid thought of destroying her came into my head, and I grasped my hands around her throat, pressed her windpipe with the thumbs, and exclaimed, 'Now I'll be the death of you', and held her so for about five minutes.

At this point Thomas demonstrated how he had positioned himself as he had strangled Mary, who had apparently only managed to utter 'Oh, Lord!' The confession continued:

> I afterwards took one of her garters off, tied it round her neck, put her into a drain, threw some grass over her, then left her. I intended reaching Edmonton on the Friday night, and on Saturday morning going to the clerk to have the banns published between myself and Maria Woodward.

When he took the stand Thomas stated that he had been disgusted with the conduct of his wife, who had not only tricked him into marriage but had picked his pocket of 35s and had been to Fenstanton with another man. He began to say that he knew it would be a sin to marry while his wife lived, but at this point in his testimony he became too agitated to continue.

The jury retired but took only five minutes before they returned the guilty verdict. The date of the execution was set for two days later, Friday 6 August, with the judge agreeing that, after pronouncement of death, the condemned man's body should be dissected and anatomised.

A few minutes after 12 p.m. on the appointed day, on gallows erected over the gateway of the county gaol, the execution was watched by large crowds. The body was then left to hang for an hour before being taken by the sheriff's officers and constables in a cart to the chemical lecture room in the botanical gardens. At about 1.30 p.m. Professor Cumming[3] began to apply electrical charges to the face and body. The audience consisted of Cambridge's medical community as well as members of the university and several respected Cambridge residents. One report of the event stated that 'The galvanic stimulus was applied to the supra-orbitary nerve (beneath the eye-brow) and the heel, when the most extraordinary grimaces were exhibited every time that the electric discharges were made – every muscle in his face was simultaneously thrown into fearful action: rage, horror, despair, anguish and ghostly smiles united their hideous expressions in the murderer's face.'

On the following day there was a public viewing of the body, and the crowd that gathered at the entrance was so large that it had to be controlled by the police.

The original grave of Mary Ann Weems. (Stewart P. Evans)

The front and back of the memorial to Mary Ann Weems. (Stewart P. Evans)

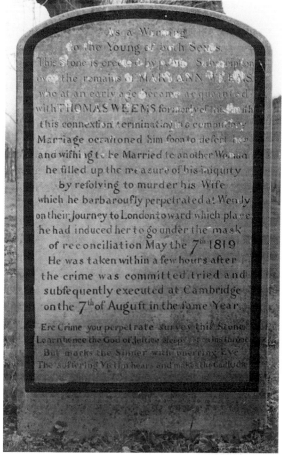

The exact burial spot of Thomas Weems remains unknown but Mary's body was displayed in the White Hart in Godmanchester before being laid to rest in the church of St Mary the Virgin, Godmanchester. Her grave was originally just marked with a small stone carved with the initials M.A.W., but later a second memorial stone was erected behind it with the words, 'To the memory of Mary Ann Weems who was murdered in the 21st year of her age' on the front and an epitaph engraved on the back.

Notes

1 A chaise is a light-weight, two-wheeled horsedrawn carriage.

2 In the *Cambridge Chronicle* the date of Mary Ann Weems's murder was reported as having taken place on 8 May, but her epitaph refers to 7 May. Other accounts refer to her as being killed on a Friday, tying in with the date of 7 May. This date therefore has been used in this account.

3 James Cumming (1777–1861) was a chemist whose research-led teaching was exemplary, in a period when laboratories were being developed and discussed. The university provided no apparatus of its own, so by his own skill he built or adapted many of the sensitive instruments required for research and lecture demonstrations.

4 Weems's execution took place on Friday 6 August 1819; the date carved on Mary's gravestone is incorrect.

5

FROM WATERHOUSE TO SLAUGHTERHOUSE

Little Stukeley is situated approximately 3 miles from Huntingdon. According to the 1821 census there were just fifty-two houses, home to 385 inhabitants. Of the families, sixteen cited their employment as handicrafts and seventy-one worked in agriculture.

The village dates back to at least the times of Richard II and was originally named Stivecle. As is typical of Cambridgeshire villages, the church is impressive, having been built and extended over many decades with several parts of the building dating to the 1600s.

It was Tuesday 3 July 1827 when the residents heard the news that their rector, the Revd Joshua Waterhouse, was dead. At first it was rumoured that he had committed suicide by cutting his own throat. The incumbent vicar for about fourteen years, the 81-year-old Revd Waterhouse was well known for both his

Drawing of Mr Waterhouse's rectory. (Norris Museum, St Ives)

meanness and his eccentricities. It was this eccentricity that made the villagers believe that suicide would not be out of character.

However, it soon became clear that there was a murderer at large.

Born in Derbyshire in 1746, Joshua Waterhouse was the youngest of four children and the son of a respectable farmer. In 1771 he entered St Catherine's Hall, Cambridge. He gained his first degree in 1774, his second in 1777 and became a Bachelor of Divinity in 1786. He was elected to a Fellowship and resided in Coton near Cambridge. Throughout his college career he was described as 'one of the handsomest and best-dressed men of his college'. His popularity with the ladies meant that by the time of his death he had amassed enough love letters to fill an entire sack. One of the women he courted was the radical feminist writer Mary Wollstonecraft, whose work included *Vindication of the Rights of Women*.

It will never be known exactly what turned Waterhouse from a popular man to the pious and eccentric 81-year-old murder victim, but J.A. Venn's *Alumni Cantabrigienses (1752–1900)* casts some light on Waterhouse's character. Venn noted that he was 'Constantly engaged in quarrels with other fellows; in 1798 voted for himself as Senior Fellow when the election to the Mastership took place; the Lord Chancellor nominated Joseph Proctor. At Little Stukeley his costume is said to have consisted of a coarse great-coat, corduroy breeches and light grey stockings.'

Although it appears that the original records no longer exist there are numerous mentions of several complaints of immoral conduct made against Waterhouse and brought before the Bishop of Ely; and that the move to Little Stukeley was an attempt by Waterhouse to put these incidents behind him.

In 1806 Joshua Waterhouse bought a parcel of land called the Denhills in Little Stukeley and paid in the region of £2,000 for the next presentation to the rectory of Little Stukeley. In 1813 the Revd Dr Torkington died and Revd Waterhouse became the incumbent of Little Stukeley, and moved there from the rectory at Coton, Cambridge. Until his death he continued to be the rector for both churches.

Once settled at Little Stukeley Waterhouse's penny-pinching ways earned him a reputation as a miserly minister. He preferred to leave his land uncultivated rather than pay the labourers a decent rate for their time. With equally false economy he hoarded any produce that he could not sell at what he felt was its correct value. This meant that every room in the vicarage, apart from the kitchen and one bedroom, was filled with either wool or grain. Many of the windows were boarded to avoid the payment of window tax and the house became so rat-infested that according to one contemporary account the vermin caused destruction 'from turret to foundation stone'.

Waterhouse lived alone, employing several villagers to work in the rectory and on the surrounding estate. On the morning of his death he had been seen at various times by several members of staff. The last person thought to have seen him alive was Ann Gale, who had arrived at the house at half past five and had then remained there until half past nine, when she had been sent to hoe thistles. She reported that the rector had appeared in good health.

The Revd Waterhouse was discovered by two of his staff, William Parker, aged 14, and Reuben Briggs, aged only 11. They had spent the morning working outside, mainly attending to Waterhouse's hogs. Between 10.30 and 11 a.m. they went into the back kitchen to have their lunch, and heard a groaning. On investigation, in the passageway leading from the back kitchen to the main kitchen, they saw Waterhouse's legs were protruding from a large brewing tub. The groaning sounds continued, and the boys were so frightened that they ran to the house of a neighbour, Ann Whitney, to seek help. Ann's immediate assumption was that Waterhouse was either drunk or playing a trick on the boys. But as they returned to their work they saw a visitor, Frederick Rogers rapping on the door with his whip in an attempt to get a response from the house. The boys told him what they had seen. After some hesitation Rogers went in and found Waterhouse as they had described.

Meanwhile the boys had summoned the help of the blacksmith, William Ashby, who, with the help of labourer William Harrison, hauled the old man from the tub. At the inquest Harrison stated that it had been half past eleven when he returned home and assisted Ashby in the removal of Revd Waterhouse from the tub, and that the body 'was then motionless, but quite warm'.

At seven o'clock on the evening of the murder William Margetts, coroner for the Hundred of Hurstingstone, began an inquest into the death. He convened the inquest at the Bell Inn with a group of respectable citizens assembled by the constable. From these a jury was sworn in. Also present were the Revd T. Brown of Conington and Henry Sweeting, Esquire, clerk of the county.

The jury was taken to the rectory where they were required to inspect the body. Witness statements were also taken. The first of these was from George Oakeley, the surgeon who had first examined the body. He stated that he had found a very deep cut near the right ear and a fracture of the right-hand side of the jaw, which had severed a large proportion of it, separating vessels with sufficient severity to cause death. He stated that a heavy weapon, such as an axe, would have inflicted the wounds and that the wounds could not have been self-inflicted.

Oakeley's evidence was supported by that of Jonah Wilson, a surgeon from Huntingdon, who, at 4 p.m., had been the next to examine the body. Revd Waterhouse had suffered at least fourteen stab wounds. There were defence wounds to his wrists and hands in addition to several more serious injuries, including one that had separated his right lower jaw, another that had severed part of his left humerus and a fatal blow to the upper part of his throat, which, according to Wilson, had 'separated the bone of the tongue from the windpipe, had penetrated the windpipe on its upper part, and completely cut across the large vessels of the neck on the right side, from which blood had spurted most forcibly, and stained the two walls of the passage in which the deed was committed'.

The boys, Parker and Briggs, were next to give evidence. Parker in particular was criticised by Sweeting for showing a lack of courage and humanity in failing to assist Waterhouse sooner. Statements were then heard from all those who had eventually come to Waterhouse's aid.

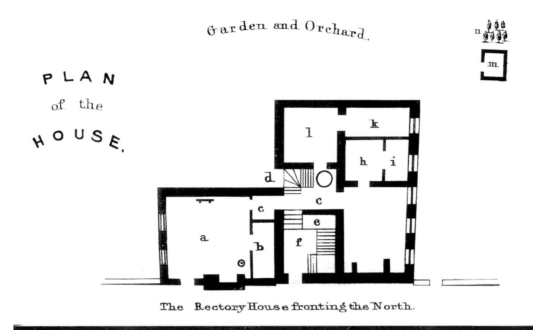

Garden and Orchard.

PLAN

of the

HOUSE.

The Rectory House fronting the North.

The floor plan of Revd Waterhouse's rectory. (Norris Museum, St Ives)
a. The Back Kitchen b. Butler's Pantry c. Passage and Back Stairs d. The Garden Door e. Closet under Best Stairs f. Entrance Hall and Best Stairs g. The Kitchen h. Small Beer Cellar i. Dairy k. Wine Cellar l. Ale Cellar m. Privy n. Plantation of young Oaks, in which the sword was found o. The Table at which Revd Waterhouse had been taking his repast O. The Tub in which the murdered body was found.
▬ The form where the boys sat to eat their luncheon.

Mary-Ann Wells of Wandsford testified on Tuesday morning, that between 10 and 11 a.m., the daughter of Ann Whitney had run to her and said 'the old man is dead', at which time Mary-Ann went to the rectory and assisted in getting him out of the tub. She recalled that his forehead was still warm and, despite a great quantity of congealed blood, Ashby had declared 'he's not dead, he's tipsy'.

William Harrison had worked for Waterhouse as a labourer for nine years and observed that both purse and keys had been left on the body and therefore the motive seemed to be revenge rather than theft.

A villager named Sarah Leach stated that she had heard a conversation connected to the case: another villager, Mrs Heddings, had remarked that on the Sunday before last her husband had noted that Waterhouse's servants had all left him and that he should not be surprised if he cut his throat 'before another Sabbath day'. Mrs Heddings was summoned from her bed at midnight. She denied any such conversation and had no suspicions of anyone.

The inquest was adjourned to the following afternoon. The parishioners had no great respect for Revd Waterhouse, and by the time the inquest reconvened at 5 p.m. on Wednesday afternoon suspicion had fallen on William Heddings and Joshua Slade. However, each produced a witness confirming that they had

Joshua Slade. (Norris Museum, St Ives)

worked in a hay field during the whole of Tuesday. Heddings' wife was recalled but again denied stating that her husband had alluded to Waterhouse's death before it had occurred.

Other witnesses were called. Anne Elby was walking near the Horse Shoes at Great Stukeley when she saw a man passing from the rectory towards the road. He headed towards the tunnel that joined the two Stukeleys, then disappeared. She arrived at the Swan at Little Stukeley at exactly eleven o'clock. Two further witnesses, Mr Francis and Mr Woods, investigated this sighting and stated that on examining the tunnel their only discovery was of footprints made by shoes with large nails in the soles.

In his summing up the coroner concluded that person or persons familiar with both the rectory and Waterhouse's habits had committed the murder and that the motive was one of jealousy or revenge. The jury returned a unanimous verdict of 'wilful murder against some person or persons unknown'.

The alibis of the two suspects were closely scrutinised. William Heddings firstly came under suspicion because he had been convicted of burglary in 1823. His sentence had been commuted to three years' imprisonment in the house of correction, but after twenty months his good behaviour had secured his early release. He returned to find that his wife had been willed a house and some money, leaving them financially secure. Despite these improved circumstances he soon returned to crime, and although he had so far avoided being caught it was well known in the village that, along with brothers John and Joshua Slade, he had been the perpetrator of numerous burglaries. Despite this, he soon proved to the coroner that he had been working in Huntingdon since the previous Sunday, and that on the Tuesday in question he had been employed by a Mr Maile to mow a field near Huntingdon.

Joshua Slade's alibi at first appeared to be equally watertight. He had been drinking at the Swan public house until one or two o'clock on Tuesday morning and from there had travelled to Godmanchester to invite his married sister to Stukeley feast. He had visited two other public houses, the Horse and Jockey, in Huntingdon, and the Rose and Crown, in Godmanchester. Apart from that he had remained at his sister's house for the whole day, returning to Little Stukeley at seven in the evening. His sister voluntarily offered a statement to corroborate his story, and Slade was released without charge.

On the Friday following the murder John Richardson, a constable of Huntingdon, apprehended Slade in order to check his alibi and accompanied him to both the Rose and Crown and the Horse and Jockey. It soon became obvious that Slade's story was a fabrication. Before long his brother-in-law, Joshua Rowledge, also retracted the statement his wife had made. Slade then amended his story, claiming that after leaving the Swan he had spent the day in a hay field sleeping off his hangover and had known nothing of the murder until his mother had told him when he returned home in the evening. He swore that he had invented the original story to protect himself from the villagers, who he was sure would try to blame him.

Slade was arrested and very soon a body of largely circumstantial evidence began to accumulate against him. The first villager to come forward was Peter Sabey, an old man who lived in a cottage opposite the rectory. Sabey claimed that he had seen a person climbing over the rectory wall at about three in the morning, and, despite the darkness at the time, asserted that the man's general appearance and distinctive gait led him to believe it was Joshua Slade.

An examination of Slade's clothes, revealed blood on the inside of the coat, and the shoes perfectly matched the footprints that had been found in the tunnel.

Another local employee volunteered that he had heard Slade saying he would murder Waterhouse and that he had keys to the rectory. Further investigation revealed that a few weeks before his death Waterhouse had been robbed during his sleep, losing approximately £2 and a pocket watch. Waterhouse had immediately suspected Slade and his sister, who had been an employee at the time and whom he immediately dismissed: it was this event that had prompted Slade to threaten Waterhouse.

Joshua Slade's family was not held in high regard in the village and a warrant was issued allowing the search of his parents' home. This was an attempt not only to prove Joshua's guilt but also to see if there was any evidence that might implicate his parents. It was noted that the house boasted a range of foodstuffs inconsistent with the family's lack of legitimate funds, but a far more interesting discovery was a cleaver stained with blood and matter that appeared to contain grey hairs. The magistrates arrested Slade's mother and father. Probably prompted by this event Joshua's brother John handed himself over to the police on the following day, admitting his robbing spree with Joshua and Heddings.

A warrant was issued for Heddings's arrest but he had already fled. On Monday 9 July 1827 a public examination took place in the Town Hall. Peter Sabey confirmed his statement that the person he had witnessed was Joshua Slade and the surgeon verified that he had found blood on the defendant's clothing. On Thursday Mr and Mrs Slade and their sons, John and Joshua, were charged with a string of burglaries linked to the items found in their home. John and Joshua confessed to these crimes, stating that Heddings was an accomplice. They were committed for trial at the assizes, while their mother and father were charged with having received stolen goods.

Late that same evening, Heddings, who had hidden in a hovel for the previous four days, handed himself in to the house of correction. He admitted burglary to Mr Sweeting and stated that Joshua Slade had confessed to him that he had murdered Joshua Waterhouse. Given Heddings' known bad character it was decided that his statement should be heard in the council chamber and in the presence of Joshua Slade. At one o'clock on Monday afternoon, Heddings made the following statement :

On Wednesday night after the murder, I saw Joshua Slade on the turnpike road in Little Stukeley, near nine o'clock. The inquest was then over. I jogged him on the elbow, and called him on one side, and asked him what he thought of this concern. He said, 'I don't know.' I made answer, 'Damn it, how came you to lay hands on him?' He said, 'I was forced; I was in the low kitchen, plundering; Mr. Waterhouse catched hold of me; I drew my knife, and began to stab him where I could; he then called out 'murder', and I got him down on the floor, and got a weapon, with which I hit him a hard blow on the face, and knocked him down; then I hit him several times on the arms, and where I could, to prevent him rising up again. I then heard the dog bark very vehemently at the door, I went to see if any person was coming; there being nobody there, I went back to Mr. Waterhouse again, and he had risen up on his legs. I then hit him another hard blow on the head, and knocked him into the tub. I then ran out at the garden door and left him. I ran down the close of grass leading to Great Stukeley.

After Heddings had completed and signed his testimony Slade was asked whether he had anything to say in response. He replied, 'No, your honour; but he has told some false tales: I did not say a word of what he says on the Wednesday night. He wants to hang me without judge or jury, damn him, he should have been hanged years ago himself.'

Before Slade was returned to prison he was questioned about a clasp knife that the prison keeper, Mr Cole, had found in his possession. The knife appeared to have some reddish-brown stains on it which Slade was asked to explain: 'They a"n't blood, nor aught like it,' he answered.

The cross-examination of Heddings continued, and in the course of all the testimony relating to the series of thefts, a man named Lansdale Wright was found to have purchased a variety of stolen items from Joshua Slade. On the evidence of Maria Sharpe, Mr Waterhouse's former housekeeper, they were identified as items taken from the rectory. Therefore, while William Heddings was far from the most reliable of witnesses, his account of Slade's confession seemed to tie in with the evidence pointing to Slade being guilty. At the very least, it corresponded with the theft from Waterhouse.

The circumstances surrounding Slade's connections to both Waterhouse and Heddings supported this. He was born on 14 January 1809 in Great Stukeley and was one of nine children. His first known meeting with Joshua Waterhouse was on 18 December 1824 when he travelled to Huntingdon to watch the hanging of a Somersham arsonist, Thomas Savage. As he approached Huntingdon, the 15-year-old old Slade happened to meet Joshua Waterhouse, and the two of them watched the execution together.

Later Slade had worked as a labourer for, among others, Mr Waterhouse. Then from November 1826 he laboured for a Little Stukeley farmer named Mr Hall. He was dismissed by Mr Hall in May 1827 after being found responsible for a petty theft. This was not the first time he had been caught stealing and he had no further regular employment, just odd days of casual work in the weeks leading up Waterhouse's death.

By this time Slade had already become close to his neighbour William Heddings. Working as a team, often with John Slade as an accomplice, they were eventually found to be responsible for a large spate of local night-time thefts, particularly those involving the rustling of livestock. The villagers of Little Stukeley had often witnessed them returning with stolen property but had kept their silence for fear of reprisals.

Heddings was a more experienced criminal. He was also an adept lock-picker and passed this skill on to Slade.

In the weeks leading up the assizes the rectory became a curiosity and was visited by many people. On Monday 30 July a huge crowd gathered in the market place to await the start of the trial. Of all the cases heard that day, only the dismissal of charges against Slade's parents and Lansdale Wright were in any way connected with the Waterhouse murder. At exactly 9 a.m. the following morning Lord Chief Baron Alexander entered the packed courtroom and Slade was brought before him. The charges were read out and when asked to plead Slade replied 'not guilty'.

There were six key points on which the prosecution based its case: the blood stains on Slade's clothes; the blood stains on Slade's knife and Sykes's bill (see page 36); the footprints found at the rectory and in the tunnel; witnesses identifying Slade by his distinctive gait; the fabrication of Slade's alibi; and the statement from Heddings.

Sergeant Storks testified that he had noticed blood on Slade's clothes when he had first interviewed the prisoner on Thursday 12 July, nine days after the killing. He stated:

> I was struck with the appearance of his trousers down the front. He wore slop fustian trousers and jacket, of a dirty brown colour, and a blue cravat; the front of his trousers, I noticed, had a dark greasy shining appearance. It struck me, but not at that moment, that it was blood and dirt rubbed together . . .
>
> I examined his jacket on the Sunday following, and his shoes three days ago; I found a large stain of blood on the inner side of the covering of the skirt of his jacket, and also a stain on the inner side of the left shoulder; the right thigh of the trousers appeared to me to have been washed, or some liquid put upon it to take out the stain.

Living as part of the Slade family was a man named Thomas Sykes, who owned a woodman's bill which he stored in a cupboard within the house. Sykes testified that the last time he had used the bill was in the spring when he had cleaned it and put it away. This became one of two possible murder weapons, the other being the clasp knife found in Slade's possession while he was awaiting trial. About this Storks stated:

> I examined the bill with a magnifying glass and could discover grey-coloured human hair and blood, and dirt appeared to have been put on afterwards. I knew Mr. Waterhouse – he was an old man, and had grey hair, and the hair on the bill corresponded. There were several cuts on the tub; they must have been given with great violence, and, in my opinion, with a bill.

The next witness to take the stand was W. Francis who had been at the Swan public house with Slade on the evening before the murder. He testified that, at somewhere between one and two in the morning, they had left the pub. The last that Francis had seen of Slade was as his drinking companion headed in the direction of both the church and his home.

On the following Monday, Francis and another man named Woods had taken one of the prisoner's shoes and gone to Mr Waterhouse's field across a stile and a ditch where, in the bank, they had found an imprint of a shoe. Comparing this to the one they carried they found it a perfect match.

When Peter Sabey took the stand his identification of Joshua Slade had become far more specific than it had been when he had made his earlier statement and included the following remark:

> The man lobbed a little in his gait, and appeared to be a young man, about five feet six inches in height. My opinion was, that it was the prisoner Slade; but I did not see his features, and could not swear it was him.

The fifth point made by the prosecution, and potentially one of the most damning for Slade, was the proof that he had fabricated his alibi and therefore had demonstrated himself to be a liar. The constable, John Richardson, took the stand and made a short but thorough statement undoing every part of Slade's original story. Joshua Slade's defence argued that as he was disliked in the village he had felt the need to protect himself from malicious gossip with the invention of an alibi.

The final evidence from the prosecution was Heddings' testimony. Despite Heddings's bad reputation his statement was the single most important element of the prosecution's case.

Heddings repeated his previous statement virtually word for word, recounting everything that Joshua Slade had purportedly told him as they walked towards the Swan public house. The judge asked Slade whether he wished to question the witness. Slade replied, 'He has told a false story, my Lord.'

When cross-examined by the defence Heddings was asked whether he thought he would be shown mercy in return for making his statement and Heddings admitted 'I hope so.'

The defence was keen to discredit Heddings as quickly as possible. Although Heddings claimed that he had been in the company of several others when Slade had confessed, no one else was able to corroborate his statement.

Joshua Slade was then invited to give his version of events:

> I saw Heddings come from the Bell, as I was in the Swan along with John Hawkes. Hawkes said, 'Tell Heddings to come in.' I went out to him and tapped him on the shoulder; he said 'What do you think of this concern?' I said, 'I don't know.'
>
> He said, 'I have a strong suspicion of old Wright.' These were his very words. He then said, 'I am sorry the old man is dead; I would as leave half

the parish had died as him, for I counted on having a quarter of barley from him this week.' Hawkes can prove that I was in the Swan, and only went out for a minute to call Heddings to have some drink.

Hawkes was called to give evidence, but did not appear.

The defence addressed each of the prosecution's points. With regards to the blood on Slade's clothes Mrs Garner clearly remembered that Slade had cut his finger and thumb while cutting bread and that this had occurred on Monday 24 June. Under cross-examination Sergeant Storks admitted, 'I said the only mark of blood I could swear to was on the left side of the trousers, and the prisoner gave a very probable cause for it'. When asked about the blood on Sykes' bill he continued, 'It is a very difficult thing to swear to blood. To the best of my belief it was human hair on the bill, and there was some stain on the handle. What I thought was human hair might have been the hair of a sheep's face, but it was not wool.'

As for the knife which had been found in Slade's possession, Wilson, the surgeon, was cross-examined and conceded: 'Other instruments of a similar shape and size would inflict such a wound. I believe the corrosion on the knife is caused by coloured animal matter; the blood of a sheep would produce the same effect.' With regards to the footprints, the Lord Chief Baron argued that as Francis and Woods had not visited the tunnel until six days after the murder it would be reasonable for Joshua Slade to have innocently travelled that route on numerous other occasions.

In his summing up the Lord Chief Baron addressed the jury. He stressed that the case predominantly rested on the statement of Heddings and that all the other evidence presented had been circumstantial. He warned the jury that Heddings's testimony was given in the same order and identically worded to the testimony he had given magistrates just over two weeks earlier and suggested that it had all the hallmarks of a prepared story. In conclusion he said that he trusted that the real criminal would soon be arrested.

By this point the general feeling was that Joshua Slade would be acquitted, but after retiring for a mere twenty minutes the jury returned the verdict of guilty. Lord Chief Baron passed the death sentence adding that Slade's 'body afterwards be dissected and anatomised'.

Immediately following this Heddings's own trial commenced. He was found guilty of theft, largely on evidence given by Joshua Slade's brother John. Heddings was also condemned to death.

John Slade was released and eventually found employment as a labourer.

On being returned to his cell the chaplain foiled Slade's attempt at suicide. Slade continued to protest his innocence, insisting that while he had been a thief he had never been a murderer. On the morning he was due to hang, Thursday 2 August 1827, the Lord Chief Baron ordered a twenty-four hour stay of execution.

On the following day the under-sheriff arrived from Cambridge with a second stay of execution deferring the execution until 1 September. During the day of 3

August Joshua Slade had said final farewells to several members of his family. Later that day he asked to see the chaplain and confessed.

The under-sheriff consulted the judges who concluded that the stay should remain in force and so should the new execution date of 1 September. The confession was written down by the county clerk, Mr Sweeting, and witnessed by Charles Margetts and John Thomas. Later Slade made an addition that he would have confessed sooner except for the thought of facing his family once they knew he was guilty.

Slade's confession clarifies all the points made in the trial:

On the morning of the 3rd of July 1827, I went direct from the Swan public house, at a quarter past two, and got over the garden wall. I was then fresh. I saw Peter Sabey at his door; I went to a straw wall near the dove-house, and laid there while five o'clock in the morning; I had a sword hid in the straw wall about four or five weeks; had stolen it from the Horse and Jockey public-house, Huntingdon; drew the sword out; and left the scabbard in the wall, and put the sword down my trousers by my thigh.

I went into the garden; saw Mr. Waterhouse then in the yard, but he did not see me; the garden door was not fastened. I opened the door, and went in up stairs and hid myself in the wool-chamber from five o'clock until ten, for the purpose of plundering the house; I meant to have robbed the house at night of any thing I could.

I was asleep from five to ten among the wool; Mr. Waterhouse, happening to come up stairs, heard me breathe; I dare say I was snoring; upon which Mr. Waterhouse came up to the chamber, and called 'Holloa! who are you? What do you do here?'

I then got up, drew the sword, and laid hold of him. Mr. Waterhouse tried to go in at the chamber where his blunderbuss was, but I would not let him. I led him down stairs, Mr. Waterhouse trying all the way to get up stairs. No conversation passed in coming down. When we got down stairs, I said, 'Now Mr. Waterhouse, if you'll forgive me, I will forgive you; and if not, this is your death warrant,' holding up the sword. Mr. Waterhouse said, 'No, I will suffer any thing first.'

I was standing opposite to him in the lower passage: When I let him go, Mr. Waterhouse went to run by me to the kitchen-door to call somebody; upon which, just as Mr. Waterhouse was turning into the kitchen, I struck him a back-handed blow, the great cut across the jaw, and he reeled back, caught himself against the tub, and fell backwards into it; he guarded his head with his hands when in the tub; I struck him several blows with the sword; he laid hold of the sword twice; upon which I drew it out of his hands and cut his fingers; I also stabbed him in the throat, which was the last blow.

Mr. Waterhouse then said, 'I am done,' and died immediately. There was no blood whatever upon me except on my finger, which I spit on and wiped it on the grass, and also one spot on my waistcoat, which I scratched out with my nail immediately; it never was seen. I have heard that blood of a murdered person will not wipe out, but I am sure this did. I did not hear the dog bark all the time; he would not bark at me; he barked once when I first got over the wall, but as soon as he heard my step he knew me, and was quiet.

The kitchen-door leading into the yard was wide open all the time; no person came into or near the house all the time. No other instrument was used, excepting the sword, and no other person was present, or knew any thing about it, until I made a confession to the Chaplain yesterday.

All that passed between Heddings and myself on the Wednesday and night of the inquest was as follows. I asked Heddings whether he would go and drink with me; Heddings drew me on one side, and asked me 'what do you think of this concern?' Heddings said, 'I have strong suspicion of old Wright, and, I am sorry he (Mr. Waterhouse) is dead; I would as leave all the folks in the town should be dead as him, for I counted of having a quarter of barley from him this week.'

Having committed the murder, which was all finished by ten minutes past ten (I had my watch with me), I immediately ran out of the house. I had pulled off my shoes when I first went into the garden at five in the morning, and am sure the footmarks alluded to in the evidence at the trial were not made then. The one in the garden might have been mine, as I was in the garden on the following day, when I was examined at Mr. Waterhouse's by Mr. Torkington. I turned immediately to the right and threw the bloody sword among the young oaks near the privy. I then ran at the back of the hay-ricks, went over that stile where it was said that the steps were, without my shoes, which I put on when I got to the top of Horse Close. In going through Dove-house Close, I saw Parker by the dove-house: but Parker did not see me. There was an old man at work in the church-yard at the same time, but he never saw me. After getting over the stile I turned to the right, and went across the closes into the tunnel; as stated in the evidence; saw the two women on the hill, did not stay in the tunnel a minute; went down the dike and laid down in Mr. Waterhouse's fields. It was about twenty minutes after ten when I got to the barley field; I remained there till seven at night; and then I went to my own house, round by the town, had my supper, and went to bed; as I was going home I saw folks running about. On Wednesday I was at work at Stanion's.

The X of Joshua Slade

Following a new search of the patch of young oaks Slade had described, the sword was discovered; and on re-inspection of the brewing tub it was clear that the damage had been caused by a weapon less crude than a bill. It is interesting that Slade's confession dismissed the prosecution's claims that the footprints, the knife and bill, the bloodstains and Heddings's statements were correct – without these points the prosecution would have had no case.

A preserved piece of skin taken from the neck of Joshua Slade and a section of the noose with which Slade was hanged. (Stewart P. Evans)

Joshua Waterhouse's grave at Little Stukeley. (Stewart P. Evans)

From the time of his confession up until his execution Slade expressed both guilt and remorse for the murder and relief at his conviction. He stated that if he had not been caught he probably would have gone on to commit further serious crimes.

On Thursday 30 August Slade had the first and only visit from his father, accompanied by two of his sisters. He spent the rest of his time in the company of the prison chaplain. On Saturday 1 September, at just after 11 a.m., Slade was placed in the cart that was to take him to the site of his execution on the outskirts of the town. A large crowd had gathered and he showed a great deal of fear until the final moments when, standing alone on the scaffold, he finally managed to compose himself.

His body was returned to the prison until it was moved for the dissection, which was scheduled for Tuesday 4 September. The medical examination revealed unusually proportioned toes explaining his distinctive gait. He had also suffered several serious blows to his head during his lifetime. A plaster mould was taken of his face. A touring museum later displayed items connected with this murder, including his skeleton. Two of the few existing exhibits are pictured: a section of the noose and a piece of preserved skin removed from the back of Slade's neck.

Joshua Waterhouse left instructions for burial: 'Let me be buried twelve feet deep – my coffin standing perpendicularly on its foot: let my face front the east: I shall then be ready: for the trumpet shall sound, and the dead shall be raised.' His grave was dug to almost that depth, but his coffin was placed in the usual position. His tomb can still be seen in the graveyard at the church of Little Stukeley but the inscription (below) is no longer legible:

> Beneath this tomb his Mangled body's laid
> Cut, stabbed and Murdered by Joshua Slade
> His ghastly Wounds a horrid sight to see
> And hurl'd at once into Eternity
> What faults you've seen him take Care to shun
> And look at home – enough's there to be done.

There is one final point of interest which makes a connection between Slade and one of the other cases in this book. The date originally set for Slade's execution – 2 August 1827 – was coincidentally the forty-first anniversary of Huntingdon-shire's previous execution, that of Gervais Matcham, whose gibbet hung nearby until it was removed just one week before Joshua Waterhouse's murder.

6
A FATAL ATTRACTION

The last public execution at Cambridge Gaol took place at noon on Saturday 13 April 1850, when two convicts were hanged for the poisoning of a young woman. What made the case extraordinary was that one of the convicts was the woman's husband and the other was her sister. But were they both guilty? Or did one just get caught up in the other's murderous plan?

Susan Reeder[1] grew up in Castle Camps, a small village in south Cambridgeshire about 3 miles from the Suffolk town of Haverhill. In 1846, at the age of 16, she married 20-year-old Elias Lucas, a strong, handsome young farm labourer whose father had been the parish council clerk in the neighbouring village of Shudy Camps. The marriage was reported as being largely a happy one, despite the fact that the couple's first child died and that three of Susan's four subsequent pregnancies resulted in the loss of the babies at or soon after birth, and that Susan suffered from respiratory problems, described at the trial as 'chest disease'.

The High Street, Castle Camps. (Cambridgeshire Collection, Cambridge Central Library)

A drawing of Mary Reeder taken from a contemporary handbill. (Cambridgeshire Collection, Cambridge Central Library)

Susan and her sister Mary were barely a year apart in age. Mary was described in a handbill produced in April 1850 as 'short and plump, and her features were even and good; the expression of her face bore the marks of innocence; her hands were remarkably white and small; and although stated in the calendar to be twenty, she seemed not more than sixteen.'

Mary, also known as Maria, had been working as a servant for Mr Miller, a carpenter and Mrs Miller, his wife. They lived in Castle End, Cambridge, very close to the county gaol. She remained in their service for fifteen months, but resigned at the end of 1849 due to ill health. Coincidentally, and like her sister, she too suffered from a bad chest. The Millers had no complaints about her work and the Cambridge locals who knew her thought her to be 'a well conducted, willing and modest girl'.

Her next position was with Mr Cross, a farmer from Castle Camps, who was also Elias Lucas's employer. At some point before Christmas 1849, while Susan was pregnant for the last time, Elias and Mary Reeder began an affair. Although it seems that Susan had no suspicions, rumours spread among the villagers, including Mr Cross, who stated, 'Maria Reeder had been in my service. I have seen the prisoners laughing and talking together near my barn. I went there and asked what they were about, and Lucas said he was helping the girl to get some kindling for the copper.'

After only a relatively short time in Mr Cross's employ Mary resigned, again stating ill health as the reason. She had the option of returning to live with her father 3 miles away, but instead she chose to live with Elias and Susan.

In January 1850 Susan's fourth pregnancy ended with the death of the child, and at Susan's suggestion Mary was invited to live with them and their surviving child, a daughter, now 3 years of age. Mary moved in at the end of January.

In spite of Susan's history of chest problems and failed pregnancies, she was reported to be in good health within a month. At the trial a local woman, Mary Wilson, said, 'I saw the deceased at 5 o'clock on Thursday, the 21st at Mr. Well's shop. She was quite well.'

On 21 February Susan shared a water mess[2] meal with her husband and sister – we do not know whether their daughter also ate with them. Neither Elias nor Mary commented on the meal, but Susan found hers tasted bitter and was soon taken ill. She continued to be violently sick through the night and the next morning. Mary gave her castor oil as a purgative, but when her condition failed to improve she went to her uncle, Thomas Reeder, in the adjoining cottage for assistance. According to his later testimony:

Maria Reeder came to my house at 10 or 11 next day, and asked me to fetch three pennyworth of brandy, for her sister was sick. Before I had finished dinner, Maria Reeder called to my wife to come and see her sister, who had fallen out of bed. She went in, and as soon as she got there she called to me out of the window to come in. I went and found the deceased on the floor in the bedroom. She was undressed. I helped to put her into bed.

Thomas sent John Casbolt to find Elias Lucas and meanwhile asked another local woman, Susan Potter, to visit his niece. The following is from Potter's account:

I went into her bedroom. She was in bed, and rose up and began to retch violently. She brought up very little, and asked me for a drink. I gave her warm tea. She drank it about three o'clock. She then began to retch again violently. I left her at 4 o'clock. She laid down in bed, and never spoke again till her husband came, about 20 minutes after I got there. She then rose up in bed, and asked him to go for a doctor. I said so too. He left the room immediately; he did not speak to his wife. I was with her when she died. She died five or ten minutes after he left the room.

Lucas rushed to his employer's house and asked Miss Cross if he could borrow a pony as he needed to fetch a doctor for his wife, although he feared she would be dead before one could reach her. Thomas Pledger, who was working on the Haverhill road about ¾ mile from the town, was the next to see Lucas. He said:

I saw Elias Lucas going for the doctor. He was on a pony and pulled up when he came to me. He was riding as fast as he could. He asked me where Mr. Robinson the surgeon lived. I asked what was amiss. He said 'my wife was taken bad after supper last night, and damn me if I do not think she will be dead before I get back'. He then went on quick. I saw Mr. Cramer coming from Haverhill in a gig. Lucas was close behind it.

A drawing of Elias Lucas taken from a contemporary handbill. (Cambridgeshire Collection, Cambridge Central Library)

Lucas went to another Haverhill doctor, Frederick Cramer, assistant to Mr Martin, because he was closest to hand and told him that Susan was desperately ill with chest pains. They hurried back to Castle Camps but as they turned into the lane they were met with the news that Susan had died half an hour earlier. Mr Cramer was about to leave for Haverhill when Henry Reeder, Susan's father, asked him to take a look at the body. Several people were at the house, including Mary Reeder, who explained that her sister had suffered with chest problems for several years. When Mr Cramer examined Susan's body her skin was still warm. To the court he later explained:

> I observed that she had died in a state of collapse. The fingers were clenched as a bird's claw. I felt the pulse and said I was sorry I was not called in before. I asked Maria Reeder if she had been purged. She said she had from a dose of castor oil given in the morning. I examined the body, and in the abdomen I found marks of recent confinement. It was supernaturally blue. These symptoms made me think the woman had died from cholera or poison. I suspected the latter.

As Cramer believed that Susan Lucas's death was not from natural causes he refused to issue a death certificate to the registrar. Perhaps in an attempt to make herself look innocent, Mary eagerly explained, 'To tell you the truth, she has been a deal worse since the water mess last night, and we all think there was something in it which caused her death. Sister first complained it tasted like slack lime, and offered me some in a spoon. I tasted it, but finding it like what sister described I spit it out. We gave some to the cat, who had also been ill.' She also said that about twenty minutes later Susan had gone to the front door, leant against the sill, and had vomited into the garden, saying, 'I am a dead woman'. Mary explained that she and Susan had prepared the food together and that the mess had not looked normal, but instead appeared curdled.

Perhaps she hoped that by explaining how she had tried the food she would not be suspected, but both she and Elias were already under suspicion. The doctor asked whether there were any poisonous substances in the house, such as corn steeped in arsenic, which could have been used as a rat poison, but Elias said no, and that in any case the bread had been bought from the baker and was not homemade.

Cramer removed what remained of the loaf and returned the following day to perform post mortem tests on the body. He found some inflammation in the chest, but overall pronounced it healthy. While the abdomen was also healthy he could immediately see that the stomach was highly inflamed. He removed the digestive tract and placed it in a bladder and a bag.

Mary told him that her sister had vomited continually through the night, and that each bowel movement had brought such pain that she had lost the power of speech.

Returning to the scene for a third time, on 24 February, Cramer met Constable Tilbrook who had been informed by Elias Lucas that there was in fact arsenic in the house. On arrival at the house Cramer asked Elias about this and was shown a large parcel on a pantry shelf, at a distance from the basins, which ruled out the possibility that it had accidentally contaminated the food. Cramer examined the parcel and found that it appeared to have been opened at one end, then loosely retied. Lucas explained that his employer had given him the packet to destroy, but that instead he had brought it home and left it in the pantry, planning, he said to put with his onion seed in order to kill slugs. It was clearly marked 'Arsenic – Poison'.

Cramer removed the rest of Susan Lucas's intestines and asked Susan's father to gather up some of the dirt outside the front door where Susan had vomited. The stomach and earth were delivered to Alfred Swaine Taylor, Professor of Chemistry and Medical Jurisprudence at Guy's Hospital, London, for further analysis.

The inquest was held at the Red Lion pub in nearby Linton. On Saturday 2 March 1850 an article in the *Cambridge Chronicle* read:

> An inquest, which has been adjourned until Monday next, was held on Tuesday on the body of a woman named Lucas, who it is suspected came by her death in a foul manner, and parties closely allied are supposed to be implicated. A portion of the contents of the deceased's stomach has been sent to Dr. Taylor for analysation, and until the adjourned inquest has taken place we refrain from more pointed or minute particulars.

On the following Saturday the next edition of the *Cambridge Chronicle* reported:

> Susan Lucas, the wife of a labourer at Castle Camps in Cambridgeshire, expired on the 22nd of February after a very short illness in the course of which she exhibited all the symptoms of having taken arsenic. A rumour

soon got abroad that the poison had been administered to her by her husband and her sister, who were reported to be on too familiar terms, the sister residing in the same house and sleeping in the same bed with the deceased and her husband.

Elias Lucas and Mary Reeder were arrested, but although both protested their innocence they were kept in custody until they could appear before Mr Justice Wightman at the Norfolk Circuit Lent Assizes held in Cambridge in March.

With the scandalous nature of the reported relationship between Lucas and Reeder, public interest was keen and the court case was reported in detail in the local press.

Professional witnesses conclusively proved that Susan Lucas died of arsenic poisoning and that the packet taken from the Lucas pantry had contained the fatal substance.

Constable Tilbrook took the stand to explain that, on delivery of the order for Mrs Lucas's burial, Elias Lucas had said that it was a bad job about his wife being poisoned. Tilbrook, in response, had asked, 'Have you any poison in the house?' Lucas replied, 'Yes, half a pound of it, or three-quarters.' He further explained that Mr Cross had asked him to dispose of it to avoid the turkeys or fowls getting at it and thereby being poisoned. He made no attempt to hide the fact that he had the poison in his possession when he spoke to Tilbrook, but Cramer testified that both Elias Lucas and Mary Reeder had denied that there was any poison in the house.

Tilbrook also confirmed that the stomach, intestines and earth had been delivered to Professor Taylor, the next witness to take the stand. An analysis of the contents revealed that the intestines were very well preserved, but both the insides and outsides were extremely inflamed, with inflammation of the oesophagus and the stomach, which was distended and contained about ten ounces of fluid. Apart from this inflammation however, there were no signs of general disease and the professor said that this was consistent with the ingestion of an irritant poison. He found black particles in the stomach lining but no food and just a small amount of digested matter in the intestines giving him the impression that violent purging or vomiting had occurred. The stomach contents comprised mucous fluid, water and arsenic amounting to two grains with further arsenic embedded in the stomach walls. He summed up his findings, saying:

> I am prepared to say that death was produced by arsenic administered to the deceased in large quantities. The symptoms are vomiting, thirst, and purging and finally collapse. The recipient of arsenic generally feels at once as if struck with death. I am clearly of the opinion that the deceased died from arsenic and no other cause.

Professor Taylor was asked to examine the parcel found in Lucas's pantry. He took a small sample for testing and applied Reinch's test, which is a common test for the detection of arsenic and produces crystals. When he returned to the stand he stated that, 'it is undoubtedly metallic arsenic, uncombined with anything. I have produced the clearest crystal.'

Mr Cross, called in to confirm that he had given the arsenic to Lucas, explained that it had been nearly a pound of arsenic and recalled 'this is the parcel I gave him. I gave it to him in the lime house in the condition in which this is. He took it away. It was a week after Old Michaelmas Day[3] I gave it him.'

Before leaving the stand he was cautioned by the judge: 'For the future I would advise you to take care how you deal with so dangerous an article as that before you. You should have seen it destroyed yourself, and I would caution you against the possession of so large a quantity,' to which Mr Cross responded that Elias Lucas had worked for him for four years and had never given him reason to think he could not trust him.

While the cause of death and the availability of arsenic were vital to the defence's case it was undoubtedly the human element that fascinated the public, and plenty of witnesses came forward with fascinating insights into the life and death of Susan Lucas.

Henry Reeder testified that his daughter Susan had persuaded him that since his wife had died Mary would be better off living with her. Reeder was in the unenviable position of giving evidence that could incriminate one of his daughters at a trial intended to bring to justice the killer or killers of the other daughter. Perhaps it was this conflict of interests that led him to speak so openly about Susan's personality. He claimed that she had had a violent temper and had often said that she would destroy herself by drowning. When cross-examined, however, he admitted that these suicidal outbursts had occurred before her marriage and that he had never heard her repeat these threats since. Elias Lucas also referred to Susan's suicidal tendencies, but said that he had dismissed the idea that his wife had killed herself, as he was sure that she would have killed him and their daughter too. She had told him that she liked the idea of the three of them dying together.

The statement of Mary Butterfield, Susan's midwife, with her account of the tragedy of Susan's lost children, touched the court. Butterfield described how Elias Lucas had returned home two hours after the birth of their last child and stated that he wished he were not married: if he had known the troubles that would come his way with marriage to Susan he would not have proceeded, even if her father had given her a dowry of £1,000. Butterfield added:

I told him not to say anything then, as it was a difficult time. This was not in the room where his wife was. He afterwards went to her room and said the same to her, I believe. He then came down and went out to work. I found his wife crying. On the Sunday after he asked me if the child was likely to live or die. I said I thought it did not look like a dying child. I went away on Monday. The deceased had a good getting-up.

Despite this, the baby had died and further rumours spread around the village that it too had been the victim of foul play. Mary Butterfield's daughter, also called Mary, took over from her mother and stayed for some days with Susan Lucas. She stated that, 'Lucas had eight pigs. I used to feed them. He came home one day in the week and said he thought the pigs grew well, and he would keep the little cad-pig (the least of the lot) till he married again, and have a green leg of pork for his dinner. He said he should marry this Mary Reeder, and went into the house. So did I.' She went on to say that Lucas told his wife he would keep this cad-pig until he married her sister. Sarah had said that it would never come to pass, for they never would allow him to marry her sister. But Mary also admitted that she had only heard him say this on that occasion and she had not thought that he sounded serious. Equally, she couldn't comment about to whom she may have repeated this story, so which of the following witnesses were genuine and which were repeating gossip is impossible to judge. It is fair to say though that some of the comments, that Lucas was reported to have made, would have been shortsighted coming from someone contemplating murder.

Two young women, Anne Ives and Emma Brown, claimed to have bumped into Lucas when they were on their way to Haverhill and said that he had told them that he had a bastard child coming, had been sick of married life from the first night and wanted to get rid of his wife, wishing she would die or go away. Both women denied seeing Mary Butterfield before their court appearances.

Elizabeth Webb, another Castle Camps resident, recounted a conversation with Lucas that initially seemed more in his favour. According to her account, he had explained how the three messes had already been made when he arrived home and that he had been told to take the largest. Mary had taken the next and his wife the remaining one. His had contained sugar, but the other two had salt and pepper. His wife had complained at the taste of hers and eventually he put it down for the cat. But instead of continuing in his favour, Elizabeth Webb reported that Lucas had commented to Susan, 'Damn it, that does not taste bad; I would eat mine if it killed me.' This was reprinted in newspaper and handbill accounts and the public were encouraged to take it as a wicked private joke shared with his lover. Lucas was further damned by public opinion when it was reported that he was full of levity during the trial, often turning towards friends in the gallery and laughing out loud when a tin box containing part of his dead wife's digestive tract was produced.

In his closing statement Mr Couch, speaking for the defence, argued that there had been insufficient motive shown, and that if the murder had been planned by both parties then the plan must have existed since the previous year when Lucas had acquired the arsenic. If this had been the case, it was inconceivable that the defendants would have been so careless in their conversations. Mr Couch asked the jury to consider whether Susan Lucas had died through self-inflicted poisoning, either deliberately or accidentally.

The jury, however, retired for only a short time before returning a guilty verdict. Mr Justice Wightman then passed the death sentence upon both the prisoners. Lucas's response was to call out, 'I am not guilty. Good bye, ladies and gentlemen. I am innocent.'

The next edition of the *Cambridge Chronicle* published a report that Mary Reeder had confessed:

All doubt as to the propriety of the verdict, and the guilt of the two wretched prisoners now awaiting execution in Cambridge county gaol upon this charge, has been set at rest by the confession of the female prisoner, Mary Reeder. Immediately after leaving the dock, this criminal became apparently resigned and penitent, and on one or two occasions gave vent to observations indicative of a desire to unburthen her mind of the load which oppressed it.

On Tuesday evening she expressed a wish to see her father and he accordingly attended on Wednesday morning, and was admitted to an interview with her in the presence of the reverend chaplain and the matron of the gaol. The presence of the chaplain appeared to act somewhat as a restraint upon her freedom of speech, so he withdrew, leaving her alone with her father and the matron; and then she acknowledged to her father that it was her hand that put the poison in her sister's mess, and attributed the desire to be rid of her to an illicit connection that existed between herself and the male prisoner, Lucas.

This connection, she said, had not taken place since Christmas last, and she most strenuously denied that she was in the family way. She has not in terms accused her partner in crime of inciting her to the commission of the deed, but she has done so by implication. She is now quite resigned to the fate that awaits her, and appears fully cognisant of the enormity of her offence.

She states that she made up her mind to commit the crime only a few minutes before its execution, and that she has not the slightest wish to live. She has paid marked attention to her religious duties. Yesterday, Good Friday, she was present in chapel in the morning, but fainted during the service and remained in her cell in the afternoon. She is constantly watched, a female attendant being with her by day and two throughout the night.

While awaiting execution she made several statements, variously saying that she alone had poisoned her sister then saying that she had committed the crime on Lucas's instruction. She claimed to have asked Lucas, 'Do you think there is any harm, Elias, in poisoning for love, as Catherine Foster[4] did?' to which he replied, 'No.' She claimed she had asked him what quantity of arsenic was needed to poison a person and he had replied, 'as much as will lie on a shilling.'

Three days before the execution Mary Reeder sent for the chaplain and in the presence of visiting justices stated that the murder was solely her doing and that Lucas had no involvement in the crime. This statement was passed to the Secretary of State, Sir George Grey, who had also received several petitions asking

William Calcraft.
(Stewart P. Evans)

for the capital sentence to be lifted. A reply eventually came on the morning of the execution: a letter arrived at the gaol to say 'that it was the opinion of the learned judge who tried the case, that both the prisoners were equally guilty, and therefore the law must take its course'.

When Lucas was informed that there would be no reprieve he replied, 'I am glad of it. I am quite prepared to die. I would not now live for £10,000. I know I shall go to Heaven if I die now; perhaps, if I were to live longer, I might not.'

Lucas and Reeder spent their last evening together, talking and strolling around the garden of the governor's house. On returning to their cells Mary went straight to sleep, suffering several convulsive fits but not actually stirring from slumber until 5 a.m. When she awoke she cried for a time and then read from the Bible.

Lucas on the other hand stayed awake, writing letters to his family and to other prisoners. The letter to his family began, 'Dear Parents, this is the last time that I shall ever communicate to you in this troublesome world, but I hope that I go to rest in God above; my dear brothers and sister and my beloved child, my own flesh and blood; but if we trust in God he will bring all things to pass.' The letters were full of religious reflection and repeated that he was ready and content to die but contained no clear admission of guilt. At 5 a.m. he drank tea then prayed until 11 a.m. when both he and Reeder received communion from Revd Mr Roberts.

Nationally, the case did not attract much attention, but locally it was a different matter; this was to be the first execution for seventeen years[5] and the crowds that assembled were the largest in living memory. The streets were reported to be full from 6 a.m. Estimates in the *Cambridge Chronicle* were probably exaggerated, putting the numbers in the region of 40,000. The gallows were erected in front of the debtor's door of the county gaol, Castle Hill, and spectators, including many women and children, gathered on the nearby Castle mound to gain a good view.

The executioner, William Calcraft,[6] pinioned the prisoners then, as the clock struck noon, they left the governor's house. Ahead of the procession was a party of javelin men, closely followed by three or four of the county magistrates, the under-sheriff and the officiating chaplain who read the burial service as he walked. Behind the chaplain walked Calcraft, followed by the officers of the gaol accompanying Lucas, then Reeder, and finally another group of county magistrates.

Lucas was first to climb up the scaffold. He appeared momentarily taken aback by the size of the crowd but, aside from that, remained calm as he took his place. Calcraft pulled the cap over his head and adjusted the rope. Mary waited at the bottom of the steps while this took place. After she had climbed Tyburn's Tree and while the rope was being adjusted around her neck Revd Roberts read the service. At its conclusion both Lucas and Reeder thanked him, saying, 'God bless you sir.' As Calcraft loosened the bolt Lucas whispered, 'I am going to God. I am going to God.'

The execution of Reader and Lucas. (Cambridgeshire Collection, Cambridge Central Library)

The execution was swift and, when their bodies had been taken down, they were buried within the precincts of the gaol.

As with other cases in this book it seems that prisoners made confessions in a suspiciously high number of cases, but Elias Lucas did not follow this trend. The final letters that Elias Lucas wrote appeared in *The Times* on 15 April 1850 and provoked an angry response which was printed shortly afterwards and goes a long way to explaining the motivation for these last minute confessions:

Sir, will you allow me a short space in *The Times* to point out what I and many others conceive to be a great abuse of the highest privilege of our religion – viz. the administration of the holy communion to criminals who die without confessing or expressing sorrow for their crimes? In the letter of Elias Lucas published in *The Times* of Monday there is no regret whatever expressed for the murder for which he was condemned by a jury of his fellow citizens and sentenced to death by one of the judges of his country. There is an abundance of advice to others, of expostulations with his parents, of remonstrances with his fellow prisoners, all tending to attract the pity and to pander to the feelings of the many morbid sentimentalists of the day; but there is not one expression conveying any sense of sorrow at having committed the crime of which he was found guilty, nor one word intimating his repentance nor his contrition at having taken the life of his wife. It is remarkable, indeed, that throughout his letters, in which he records his affection for his parents and child, he does not say one word of kindly allusion to her whom he had once sworn to love and to cherish, and whom he afterwards murdered; and yet this man is allowed to participate, at the eve of his execution, in an office which abounds with invitations to repentance, and which prohibits any to appear but those 'who truly and earnestly repent of their sins'.

I do not maintain that every criminal is to be excluded from the holy communion, but certainly in no case should this sacrament be administered to a murderer, unless he prepare himself for a due participation in that rite by a confession of his crime and by expressing a deep sorrow for the perpetration of it, and a hearty and true contrition at having injured and murdered a fellow human being. This practice of admitting murderers to the holy communion, without a previous confession and repentance, is only of late adoption, and I hope you will admit this protest against it ere it become a custom, which, if once established, will prove injurious to society, revolting to pious minds, and tending to bring religion into contempt. I am, Sir, your obedient servant,

CLERICUS.

Clearly the clergy preferred prisoners to lie and make a false confession rather than keep their silence. Although Lucas believed in God and knew death was imminent he continued to claim that he was innocent.

Various comments that he had made while awaiting execution were printed in the *Cambridge Chronicle*: 'The male prisoner still denies that he was aware of the intention of Mary Reeder to poison his wife. He admits that an improper intercourse had taken place between himself and his fellow prisoner, and states that it subsisted up to within about six weeks of his being taken into his custody. He adds that he had become disgusted with Mary Reeder and was determined to be rid of her; and that if he could have but succeeded in effecting that, he should have lived happier with his wife for the future. Some time before the death of his wife, Mary Reeder asked him for some arsenic to put in the water in which she said she was about to bathe her feet, and said that she thought it would cure her chilblains; he gave her some accordingly.'

And later, 'With regard to the death of his wife, he says he believes himself morally to be as guilty as the female prisoner, as it was her connection with him that led her to the commission of the crime.'

While stopping short of admitting any responsibility for the act of planning and carrying out the murder of his wife, Elias Lucas was burdened with guilt. The *Cambridge Chronicle* printed another statement he made to Revd Roberts: 'I do recollect what Mary said to me, "Elias, do you think there is any harm in poisoning anybody for love?"' He then recounted the rest of the conversation just as Mary had explained it. Later he said to Revd Roberts, 'Well I might have told her to do it, but if I did, it was when I was in a passion.' He said on numerous occasions that he ought to die for having been intimate with his wife's sister, but also insisted that he had no knowledge of the crime Mary was to commit.

Clericus' letter to *The Times* complained that Elias Lucas had made no mention of his wife in his last written words, but a handbill produced in the days after the execution stated that: 'The prisoner had never breathed one word against her, but acknowledged she had been a kind, good-hearted, and unsuspecting woman.'

It was possibly unfortunate for Lucas that he and Mary Reeder were tried jointly and shared a defence; the question of only one of them being guilty was never raised. The evidence against Reeder was substantially stronger than any evidence against Lucas but in order to defend them jointly, their counsel, Mr Couch, had to ask the jury to accept the improbable scenario that Susan Lucas had poisoned herself. In light of the scandalous relationship that had existed between the defendants, acquittal was not an outcome the jury were likely to reach.

The scenario of Lucas conducting a rash affair with Mary while his wife was alternating between illness and pregnancy is not far-fetched. Once the affair had ended his motive for murder was far more obscure than Mary's. Had he not been in possession of the poison, if Mary had acquired it from elsewhere or if it had come from an unknown source then the major part of the evidence against him would have not existed.

Notes

1 Reeder was also spelt 'Reader' in many accounts but I have chosen the former as it appears to be the more frequently used.

2 Water mess is made from crumbled bread, water, pepper, salt and either butter or dripping.

3 Michaelmas Day, 29 September, is the feast of St Michael the Archangel, and one of four quarter-days in England.

4 Catherine Foster, née Morley, lived near Sudbury in Suffolk and was executed for poisoning her husband in 1846. She had married a man her mother had chosen but she was in love with someone else. After just three weeks of marriage her husband died from arsenic poisoning and Catherine pleaded guilty. She was the last woman to be hanged in Suffolk and was just 18 when she died.

5 John Stallon, known as the Shelford Incendiary, was executed after setting twelve out of thirteen fires that had occurred in Shelford in the early 1830s.

6 William Calcraft executed between 400 and 450 people between 1829 and 1874, making him the longest serving and most prolific of executioners. He had the reputation, however, of miscalculating the drop, so that many of the condemned were strangled to death.

7
THE ONE SHILLING KILLING

Newmarket Road is a long road leading into Cambridge from the east, which changes its name to Maids Causeway as it nears the city centre. In the nineteenth century its local nickname was Coarse Maid's Way, as it was well known as a thoroughfare along which prostitutes would walk to the red light area. Along Maids Causeway was a junction known as Four Lamps. It was near there that two prostitutes, Emma Rolfe and Annie Pepper, met a young tailor named Robert Browning on the evening of Thursday 24 August 1876.

Browning was in his early twenties, with various reports stating that he was between 23 and 25, but was said to look much younger. He was also described as

The area of Cambridge known as Four Lamps. (Cambridgeshire Collection, Cambridge Central Library)

having 'an imperfect education' and had been discharged from the 9th Regiment with a bad character reference. Since his discharge he had worked with his brother at a shop in Covent Garden in the Mill Road area of Cambridge. The brothers lived with their parents but Browning chose to spend most of his free evenings drinking and paying for the company of prostitutes.

The brothers' latest commission had been to make a pair of trousers for a local businessman named Mr Ward. This client had offered to pay them extra if they finished on time and, once their work was completed, the brothers headed off for the evening. It was about 8.30 p.m. when Browning left his brother and went home for supper. He seemed preoccupied and ate little. His mother suggested that he would be better off staying in for the rest of the evening but Browning took no notice. Instead he slipped a cut-throat razor into his coat pocket and left the house.

First he went to Fair Street and into a pub called Canham's then, at 9.30 p.m., met with the two young prostitutes, possibly by prior arrangement. He was not interested in both of them, so Pepper departed and Browning was left alone with Rolfe, who was only 16 years old but who had been living in a brothel for the previous few weeks. A Mrs Phillips owned the brothel, which was situated in Crispin Street.

With the promise of a shilling Rolfe willingly accompanied him into the darkness of Midsummer Common. Within moments he had taken out his razor and sliced open her throat. Her death was almost instantaneous but, some way across Midsummer Common, Constable Joseph Wheel heard a single shriek.

The Garrick Inn, Cambridge. (Cambridgeshire Collection, Cambridge Central Library)

A drawing of Emma Rolfe taken from a contemporary handbill. (Cambridgeshire Collection, Cambridge Central Library)

Browning left her body where it fell and returned the bloodied razor to his pocket. Despite his bloody and dishevelled state he walked to the nearby Garrick Inn and drank a quick glass of ale. On his departure he ran into PC Wheel who was searching for the source of the scream. Browning immediately handed himself over but was not taken seriously until he had taken the constable onto the Butts Green area of Midsummer Common and exposed Rolfe's body. The wound in her neck was so enormous that her head was almost severed. Browning's explanation was that she had tried to steal a shilling from him. He showed Wheel the murder weapon.

Browning said, 'I just killed the girl. Don't let me look at her. Take me away from her. Don't look at her.' And a little later he added, 'I hope the poor girl is in Heaven. I did not give her much time to repent.' He was also concerned about the effect his crime would have on his mother.

Mr Southall, a lodger at the Garrick Inn, joined PC Wheel and together they took Browning to the police station.

Rolfe's body was taken to the Fort St George public house where an inquest was held the following day. Her father, James Rolfe, a hawker living in Leeder's Row, identified the victim's body. He explained that she had moved out of his house and claimed not to know where she had lived since. When he explained that they no longer spoke when they saw one another it was clear that they had fallen out.

Mr Robert Roper, a surgeon of Cambridge, described the body:

On the night of Thursday, the 24th of August, a few minutes before ten, I was sent for to go to the Common where I found a woman lying on her left side with her throat cut and quite dead. In half a minute's time a policeman came up and showed us his light. It was intensely dark but I knew the woman was dead before he arrived. On examining the body, I found the head and hands cold but the arms were warm. The woman had been dead very few minutes. It was an extensive wound from the left to the right, quite down through everything to the spinal column. It was the largest wound of the kind I ever saw. It was high up in the throat under the chin. Such a wound might have been given by a razor and would cause immediate death. I believe the woman was lying on the ground. I don't believe a person would have inflicted the wound on the woman while she was standing. Great force must have been used in inflicting the wound.

After hearing other statements from police and other witnesses the jury at the inquest returned a verdict of 'Wilful murder by Robert Browning'. On 29 August Browning was brought before the mayor of the borough and committed for trial. He was sent to Norwich Gaol to await the winter assizes, which were to take place in the city in November.

During his trial his mother testified that he had appeared 'very gloomy and strange' since coming home after his army discharged. She also explained that:

he was very ill and went into Addenbrooke's Hospital, but I did not know with what complaint. When he came out of the hospital he appeared to be strange and gloomy. He sulked and did not take his food. This strange appearance increased up to the time of this occurrence. There was a great change in him since Midsummer Fair. My bedroom was close to his. At night I have heard him very restless and often out of bed.

It was also established that there was a history of insanity in other male members of Browning's family.

The biggest clue to the motive for the murder came from Mr James Hough, surgeon to the gaol, who stated:

I have frequently seen the prisoner, who was suffering from a contagious disease when he was taken into custody. He was in a very bad state. Under my care he has, to a certain extent, recovered. I saw the prisoner nearly every day, and I have had the opportunity of observing his conduct. I never saw anything in his mind, manner and acts to lead me to suppose that there was anything wrong in his mind. I am not aware that a chronic state of the disease from which he was suffering has a tendency to weaken the brain. The disease, so far from affecting the brain, was of a purely local nature.

A contemporary street ballad about Emma Rolfe and Robert Browning. (Cambridgeshire Collection, Cambridge Central Library)

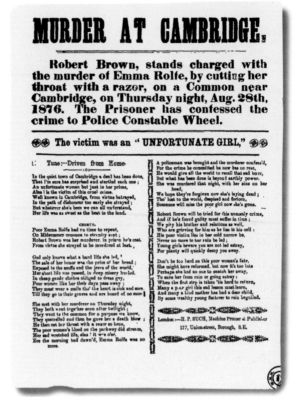

When Browning eventually revealed his motive for murdering Rolfe it transpired that she had just been an unfortunate victim of circumstance. Browning had held a grudge against prostitutes since catching an incurable venereal disease from an encounter in Royston. It was in fact this girl, who he referred to as 'Miss Bell', that he had wanted to kill.

On 29 November Browning was found guilty. Although he made very little effort to defend himself the jury showed some sympathy and asked the judge, Mr Justice Lush to consider sparing him the death penalty on the ground of his youth. Justice Lush, however, saw little reason for leniency and included the following words as he passed sentence: 'The law, however, is more humane than you were. You felt immediately afterwards that you were taking the girl's life away without the slightest opportunity for repentance or preparation. You will have time, and I hope and pray that you will make use of the time which the law allows you, in order to prepare for that event . . . I shall take care to convey the recommendation of the jury to the proper quarter; but I cannot hold out any hope that the recommendation will have any effect.' After sentencing Browning was transferred to Cambridge Gaol.

Browning was interviewed by the Inspector of Prisons, Dr Briscoe, and given the chance to put forward his case. The inspector's report concurred with Justice Lush's sentence and its findings were passed on to the Home Secretary.

The sentence stood therefore. Shortly before 8 a.m. on 15 December 1876 Browning was led to the gallows. Before his execution he made a full confession which included the following statement: 'Having promised the girl a shilling, we walked together on to the common and scarcely spoke a word, when, without provocation on her part, I committed the foul deed, feeling at the moment that I must take away the life of some one.'

According to *The Times*:

He slept comfortably during the night, and rose a little after 6 o'clock, when he partook of breakfast – bread and butter and cocoa. He walked from his cell, accompanied by the chaplain and officials, to the scaffold with a firm step but crying and sobbing. At 8 o'clock the bell of St Paul's Church and that of the prison announced the fatal hour. The prisoner said nothing, but listened to the chaplain. Marwood, with his usual expedition, performed the execution, and in a minute or two the unhappy man ceased to live. He was heard to exclaim 'Oh!'

Marwood had allowed a drop of 6ft 10in because Robert Browning was of 'light stature'.

Browning was the first person to be executed within the walls of Cambridge Gaol. Several street ballads were composed and this is the chorus of one:

> Poor Emma Rolfe,
> Thy fate was dreadful,
> For vengeance now,
> Your blood it cries.
> We hope your precious soul's in heaven,
> Far away in your blue skies.

And this, to the tune of 'Driven from Home', was circulated while Browning was in gaol awaiting trial:

> Poor Emma Rolfe had no time to repent
> On Midsummer Common to Eternity sent
> Robert Brown (*sic*) was her murderer, in prison he's cast
> From virtue she strayed to be murdered at last.

8

'TIS
QUITE HARMLESS

At the time of his conviction the *Daily News* described Walter Horsford as 'the greatest monster of our criminal annals'. It had not taken long for him to gain the soubriquet of 'the St Neots Poisoner' despite his never having lived in the town. Although he was arrested and convicted of just one murder, he was suspected of committing at least two more. Even before his arrest in 1897, there had been rumours that he was responsible for some sudden and unexplained deaths in the area.

He was born in 1872 and as a teenager lived with his parents in Stow Longa, a small village situated just outside Spaldwick. By the early 1890s Horsford was described as 'a respectable farmer' who tilled land not far from his home. In 1897 he was having an affair with one of his first cousins, Mrs Annie Holmes, who was twelve years his senior. She had been married to a coal and corn merchant from a village just outside Thrapston in Northamptonshire, but was widowed in the mid-1880s at the age of 25. For two years, until October 1897, she lived in Stoney, near Kimbolton, Huntingdonshire with her son Percy and daughter, also called Annie. While at Stoney she gave birth to another son but it is not known who his father was.

Horsford was a fairly frequent visitor, but on 14 October Mrs Holmes moved her family to rented accommodation in East Street, St Neots. It is not known what prompted the move, but just twelve days later, on 26 October 1897, Horsford married a young woman named Bessie.

A drawing of Annie Holmes. (St Neots Advertiser)

The relationship between Holmes, now 38, and Horsford, was almost at an end, although he did make at least two visits to her at her new address. During December she wrote to inform him that she was pregnant. In his reply he advised her to see a Dr Mackenzie at Raunds. Although she wrote to this doctor she does not appear to have visited.

At the turn of the year Horsford contacted her again, this time by letter, which she received on 5 January. He wrote:

> Dear Annie, Will come over Friday to see you if I can come to an arrangement of some sort or other, but you must remember that I paid you half a crown, so if I thought well not to give you anything you could not get it, but still, I don't want to talk and hear that it is by me, if you really are so.
>   Don't write any more letters as I don't want Bessie to know.

On the day of the arranged meeting, 7 January 1898, Holmes seemed anxious. Her daughter said she seemed as though she were waiting for something, but instead of a visit from Horsford she received a letter. In the evening Holmes fed her children (Percy now aged 15, Annie 14 and the baby aged 1) and went to bed with the baby. As she had spent the day feeling unwell she took a glass of water with her.

Mother, daughter, and baby shared a bed, and when young Annie joined her mother she noticed that the glass standing on the chest of drawers was virtually empty. Her mother still did not feel well and asked her daughter for a 'sweetie' which she sucked upon. A short time afterwards, probably within the next twenty minutes, Holmes's daughter noticed that her mother was ill, 'struggling and kicking as if suffering convulsions'. Firstly the neighbours, Mrs Fisher and Mrs Ashwell, were called and then Percy ran for the St Neots doctor, Joseph Herbert Anderson.

Dr Anderson found Holmes suffering convulsions, with her face and lips livid and her eyes strained and rolled up towards the ceiling. Dr Anderson later explained that his instant assumption was that she had been poisoned and he therefore asked her what she had taken.

She replied, 'I have taken a powder to procure an abortion.' She continued to reply to his questions between convulsions and despite her pain she was totally coherent and added: 'I believe I am poisoned.'

The doctor prepared an antidote but Holmes died before it could be administered. Although it was the first case of strychnine poisoning[1] he had seen he was immediately clear that it was the cause of the symptoms. The antidote he prepared was choral and bromide of potassium. Although he knew she was about to die he hoped that he might be able to alleviate some of her symptoms.

The police were contacted and, at 11.40 p.m., John Allen Purser, an officer from St Neots, arrived and spoke with the victim's daughter. He decided to search the house and started, aided by a Sarah Hensman, in the bedroom. Almost immediately they found a plain sheet of paper under the head of the bed.

Moving through the house, Purser found seven packets of Dover Powders[2] that Holmes had kept in her workbasket downstairs. On completion of his search, at approximately 1.30 a.m., he locked the house and left it empty, returning at 10 a.m. the following morning. He searched the bed as well as he could without disturbing the body but despite lifting the mattress discovered nothing else. He left again at 11.15 a.m. leaving young Annie and a Miss Mary Agnes Busby in the house. He arrived back at 2 p.m., shortly before Dr Arthur Cromac Turner, a St Neots surgeon, who was to undertake the post mortem.

Doctors Anderson and Turner carried out the post mortem where it was confirmed that Holmes had died from strychnine poisoning. All her organs were in good health and she was found to be not pregnant.

The inquest was held the same day. The coroner was Charles Robert Wade-Gery. Dr Anderson gave his findings, which were corroborated by Dr Turner.

One of the witnesses called was Horsford, whose signed deposition stated: 'I live at Spaldwick. Cousin of the deceased. Have known her all my life. I have never written to her all my life or sent her anything either by post or messenger. I have been to see her twice since she lived at St Neots, but there has been no familiarity between us at any time.'

However, on the 8th, when Holmes's body was being laid out, three papers were discovered under the mattress. One was the letter Annie had received on 5 January, the second was a packet with the words 'One dose, take as told', and the third a note which said, 'Take in a little water; 'tis quite harmless. Will come over in a day or two and see you.' All three papers bore Horsford's handwriting and the packet contained no fewer than 30 grains of strychnine.

On Sunday 9 January Constable Elmore joined Purser at Holmes's house. They made another search, but no other poisons were found. The only unidentified substance in the house turned out to be baking powder; it appeared that the strychnine could only have come from the packet under the mattress. Purser was also present at the inquest and when the inquest statement was read out and signed by Horsford.

On Monday 10 January the coroner issued a warrant for Horsford's arrest. Purser drove to the accused's farm at Spaldwick and detained him on a charge of wilful and corrupt perjury. Purser said, 'I hold a warrant for you for perjury at the inquest on Annie Holmes on the 8th inst.'

Horsford replied, 'Perjury : I don't know what it means.'

'It means you told a lie when giving your evidence.'

'I don't understand it.'

As Horsford was cautioned, Bessie said: 'I believe it is all about that woman Annie Holmes,' and then asked whether her husband would be able to come home again that evening. Purser was non-committal but said that he hoped it would be possible.

However, Horsford remained in custody and, at St Neots Police Court[3] on 27 January, he was brought before magistrates having been charged with both perjury and wilful murder. Holmes's body had been exhumed from Stow Longa

Walter Horsford drawn by a Leader *artist.* (The Leader)

on 26 January and a Home Office analyst, Dr Thomas Stevenson, was conducting experiments on the organs with the assistance of Dr Anderson. Because of the nature of the tests Dr Stevenson warned that it would take up to a month for the results to be available. The case therefore was adjourned.

The case finally came before the south-eastern circuit Assizes on 2 June. The judge was Mr Justice Henry Hawkins, with Mr J.F.P. Rawlinson, Q.C. and Mr Raikes standing for the prosecution and Mr E.E. Wild and Mr Barrett presenting the defence.

Dr Stevenson's results were made public at the second day of the Assizes, on 2 June 1898. From the stomach contents he had extracted 1.31 grains of strychnine. He had conducted multiple tests – including testing some of the poison on animals – but no other toxins had been detected. The paper marked 'one dose, take as told' held 33.75 grains and another paper marked with blue and red lines also showed traces of strychnine.

The exhumation of the body had occurred nineteen days after death and there was rigidity in the fingers and lower limbs which in his experience was another clear indication of strychnine poisoning. He confirmed that all the organs appeared healthy, although all also contained the poison. By his calculations this meant that Holmes had consumed somewhere between seven and twelve grains of strychnine although the 1.31 grains found in her stomach would have been a fatal dose. He confirmed that the victim had not been pregnant either recently or at the time of her death.

He stated that he could imagine 'no more terrible mode of death' than by strychnine; the afflicted person remained in complete possession of their faculties and normally died within thirty minutes after the onset of the symptoms, but in an extreme case up to six hours later. Death would either occur through exhaustion or suffocation caused by the chest going into spasm. If taken in water most of the poison would have settled and a smaller quantity would have remained suspended in the liquid. Once drunk it would circulate in the victim's system very quickly and one of the first symptoms would be stiffness in the back of the neck followed by spasms.

Under cross-examination by the defence he admitted that it was not uncommon for pregnant women to use strychnine in an attempt at abortion or suicide, although he stressed that strychnine could never be a successful way to produce an abortion.

The first of the neighbours called as a witness was Mrs Fisher, who along with Mrs Clara Ashwell had gone to the house at the request of Holmes's children. Although Fisher had been unable to stay for long she had seen that Holmes was in deep distress, writhing around and shouting. At one point, according to her testimony, Holmes had called out to her daughter, 'I am so bad.'

Ashwell confirmed this, adding that Holmes had cried, 'rub me'. Clara had sent the daughter Annie downstairs with the glass to fetch more water and had sent Percy to fetch brandy and a doctor. Ashwell had been unable to give the unfortunate Holmes any brandy as her teeth had been too tightly clenched. After the arrival of the doctor Ashwell had gone downstairs to mix some mustard and water but, by the time she returned, Holmes had died. Another local woman, Sarah Hensman, was present in the room when Holmes passed away.

Constable Purser was called to give evidence and explained how, from the evening of Holmes's death, he made several searches of the house. Mr Wild, defending, cross-examined Purser. He was critical of the number of visitors allowed entry to the crime scene and demanded to know who had had access to the house after Holmes's death. Purser stated that he had been the last to leave in the early hours of 8 January, and a key had been given to Mrs Sarah Ann Bull. In the morning Mrs Bull handed the key to Miss Busby.

Sarah Hensman testified that she did not visit the house again until between 8 and 9 on the morning of the inquest when she had returned with Mrs Gale to lay out the body. They had moved the body to the edge of the mattress with Gale being around the far side of the bed pulling out the two feather mattresses from between the body and the palliasse.[4] It was then that they noticed some items lying directly underneath where the body would have lain. Hensman noticed that there were two packets and some letters and she left them all on the chest of drawers. She went downstairs to Mr Benjamin Horsford Mash, Holmes's brother, who came up to the bedroom and read the letters. Despite drawing her attention to the powder in the packet she did not actually see it until shown by the coroner.

Benjamin Horsford Mash appeared as a witness for the prosecution. He was of course Walter Horsford's cousin and not only knew the accused's writing but had with him a receipt in his script. He had arrived at Holmes's house during the day following her death when Constable Purser, Percy Holmes, Mary Busby and Laura Horsford, another cousin of Walter's, were present. Apart from locking away some silver, he touched nothing. It was a little later when Hensman showed him the letters and papers found under the mattresses. He read them and saw that they were from his cousin. Mash took them to the police station and handed them over to Superintendent Freestone.

Under cross-examination Mash admitted that he had been on bad terms with Horsford. His last correspondence with his cousin had been a letter, about a number of sheep, received two years earlier.

In order to verify further that the writing on the notes was Horsford's, William Conney, the stationmaster from the Great Northern railway station at Huntingdon, was called. He produced two recent letters from Horsford, both of which were signed. From Huntingdon a builder named John James Row was also called. Although he had received and subsequently destroyed a letter from Horsford he was shown some blotting paper removed from Horsford's house, which bore a mirrored copy of the letter, and he was able to confirm that the writing belonged to the accused.

Thomas Henry Garrin, a Fellow of the Royal Microscopical Society and a specialist in handwriting, was called as an expert witness. In his opinion the writing on the 'coming over on Friday to try and make an arrangement' letter and the packets marked 'Take in a little water; 'tis quite harmless' and 'One dose, take as told' were all of the same hand. The writing was natural and had been written rapidly without any attempt to disguise it. He compared these items of evidence with the writing in the letters to Mash, Conney and Row as well as with three signatures on paperwork for removing swine from a swine-fever area. Garrin testified that every item put before him had been written in the same hand. In his view, Horsford had written all of them.

Under cross-examination, Mr Wild, defending, drew Garrin's attention to several areas where the handwriting appeared to differ, but Garrin argued that his fourteen years' experience of handwriting put him in the position where he frequently gave opinions that did not agree with untrained judgements and that he had no doubt in this case that every example shown was Horsford's.

When Superintendent Freestone took the stand he explained that he had been suffering from whooping cough on the night of Annie Holmes's death so he had sent Constable Purser. After the inquest he had sent a jar found at Holmes's house to Dr Stevenson, which was found to contain only baking powder. On 8 January Mr Mash had brought around a variety of papers that had been found under his sister's mattress and which he had sent to the analyst, Mr Knight, at Cambridge and then delivered back to Dr Stevenson.

Superintendent Freestone had visited chemists in St Ives, Huntingdon and St Neots and had checked their poison registers. These visits drew a blank so he cast his net wider and the following day visited Mr Payne, a chemist at Thrapston where he discovered a record of the poisons bought by Walter Horsford. He also found that other farmers commonly bought large quantities of pure strychnine and, when mixed into a compound known as 'rattles', it was an efficient rat killer.

Next he checked the previous four years' sales of poisons with chemists in Kimbolton, Raunds, Thrapston, Oundle, Peterborough, Huntingdon, St Ives and St Neots and found that no strychnine had ever been sold to the accused's wife.

On 10 January he obtained a search warrant for Horsford's house where a letter and some blotting paper were recovered.

The court then heard testimony from Joseph Hind Payne, the Thrapston chemist.

On 28 December 1897 Horsford had purchased arsenic, strychnine, prussic acid and carbolic acid from him. Thrapston was about 12 miles from Horsford's home which, in the days before motorised transport, was considered some distance.

As required by the Pharmacy Act the chemist kept a poison book, which was signed by Horsford and showed that he had purchased a drachm[5] and a half of strychnine (90 grains), a pound of arsenic and an ounce of prussic acid, equating to a shilling's worth of each. The strychnine was in the form of powder, not crystals. Payne stated that each packet had been clearly labelled with the word 'POISON' in red ink. As the chemist did not know Horsford, under the Pharmacy Act another witness was required. Horsford had gone into the street and spotted Walter Pashford of Catworth, a farmer, who was known to both him and the chemist. Pashford witnessed the purchase, then the two men had left the shop together. It was never known whether Horsford's meeting with Pashford had been accidental or pre-arranged. When Pashford was called he testified only that he had indeed been the one to introduce Walter Horsford to Joseph Payne.

Holmes's daughter, still only 14, stated that on 5 January, two days before her mother's death, there had been a knock at the door and she had found a letter in the letterbox. It was addressed to her mother and was in handwriting that she recognised as Horsford's. She also noted that it bore a Huntingdon postmark, but that unusually her mother did not let her read the letter. She also identified the writing on one of the packets found under the mattress as Horsford's.

Young Annie was downstairs when her mother died. She washed out the glass that her mother had drunk from. It was unusual for her mother to take water to bed but she stated that she had not noticed anything unusual about the dregs of water that remained in it.

When cross-examined she said that she was positive that she was able to identify Horsford's handwriting. She was also aware that her mother kept powders in a workbasket, although she had never been known to take any as, apart from the occasional bout of neuralgia,[6] she was in good health.

Under cross-examination she was also pressured to admit that another of her mother's relatives, William Mash, had been a frequent visitor to their house at Stonely. He had sent money and continued to visit after the birth of the younger son.

In their summing up, on 5 June, the prosecution and the defence were quite different in their approaches. In fact, throughout the trial Mr Wild, the defence counsel, had been astonishingly reluctant to call and cross-examine witnesses, although he did cross-examine Holmes's daughter in an attempt to prove that her mother had been a 'woman of loose and profligate character'. Paraphrasing Horsford's letter Wild commented that his client had no reason to murder a 'woman that he valued at half-a-crown'.

The prosecutor, Mr Rawlinson, in his closing statement delivered a clear and logical summary of the evidence. He argued that the 'arrangement' letter proved that Horsford was keen to keep both the affair and the pregnancy secret from his new wife. No one disputed that the victim had died from strychnine poisoning or that she had access to the substance. There also appeared to be no reason why Holmes would have taken it deliberately. As the packet labelled 'Take in a little

Annie Holmes's daughter, also Annie, drawn by a Leader *artist.* (The Leader)

water; 'tis quite harmless' was found under the bed, he argued that it was reasonable to assume that she had trusted the instruction and taken the powder it contained. Whoever had written the instruction and sent the packet had clearly wanted her dead; the only person shown to have a motive was Horsford.

Both Holmes and Mash, neither experts, had identified the handwriting, but so too had Garrin and he was an expert in the field of handwriting identification.

Horsford had admitted purchasing 90 grains of strychnine on 28 December 1897, and the evidence proved this. Although he denied murder, he had been unable to demonstrate where those 90 grains had been used.

Wild's summing up was notably weaker; he argued that the case against Horsford rested on nothing more than prejudice and elaboration, that the letter bore a Huntingdon postmark but not a second Spaldwick one and that the identification of the handwriting was unreliable. He did not include any evidence that could establish his client's innocence. In fact he pointed out to the jury that 'if one jot or tittle of evidence had been put forward, or a single document put in he would lose the last word on behalf of the prisoner'.

Justice Hawkins later commented: 'Of course, counsel's last word may be of more value than some evidence; but the smallest "jot or tittle" of evidence, or any document whatever that even *tends* to prove the innocence of the accused, is of more value than a thousand last words of the most powerful speaker I have ever listened to. And I would go further and say that evidence in favour of a prisoner should never be kept back for the sake of the last word. It is the bounden duty of counsel to produce it, especially where evidence is so strong that no speech could save the prisoner.'

The defence concentrated its efforts on attacking the character of Holmes and also pointed out that, at the time her death, Horsford had been miles away at the Falcon Hotel in Huntingdon.

The court was adjourned overnight. On its reconvening Justice Hawkins began his summing up, firstly making it clear to the jury that if they decided that Horsford had deliberately encouraged Holmes to take the poison, whether or not his intent was to kill her, then it was murder. Even if the intention was only to procure an abortion and death resulted from the taking of poison, it was still murder.

The judge castigated the defence for the cross-examination to which the victim's daughter had been subjected and emphasised that there was nothing to suggest that Holmes had not been living a poor but decent life. He added: 'It more than pained me when I heard the learned counsel – instructed by the prisoner – cross-examine that poor little girl, left an orphan by the death of the mother, with a view to creating an impression that the poor dead creature was a person of shameless character.' The judge was satisfied that Holmes had received Horsford as a visitor before his marriage, and had then moved to St Neots. The judge also said that it was beyond doubt that Horsford had lied at the inquest, that he had written the letters and that Holmes believed herself to be pregnant. He said that her supposed pregnancy should be considered sufficient motive for her murder.

He said that Horsford's appearance at the Falcon Hotel coincided with the date he had promised Annie that he would visit and, rather than being in his favour, it was suspicious that he had made sure he was nowhere nearby. Also suspicious was the fact that the accused had never gone to his victim's house after her death to pay his respects.

The judge queried the defence's strategy noting that, 'the learned counsel had been content with vague surmises without a shadow of evidence to support them.' Finally he concluded that the strychnine bought by Horsford was responsible for Holmes's death so all that remained was for the jury to decide whether Horsford was responsible for her taking it.

While the case had lasted for five days and the judge's summing up for two and a half hours the jury returned after only twenty-five minutes with a verdict of guilty. Horsford was asked by the Clerk of Arraigns if there was any reason why he should not receive the death penalty and he simply replied: 'All I can say is that I am an innocent man.'

Justice Hawkins placed the black cap on his head and sentenced Horsford to death.

Later that day Horsford was transferred by closed carriage to Chesterton prison, 14 miles away, where he was to await execution. His execution was at 8 a.m. on Tuesday 28 June 1898 at Cambridge gaol where the hangman, James Billington, calculated that a 7ft drop would be required. According to a report in *The Times* Horsford 'walked to the execution chamber firmly and apparently unconcerned'. The chaplain said a prayer and Horsford's death was instantaneous.

Just after his execution this notice appeared in *The Times*:

The St. Neots Murderer. We are requested by the Home Office to state that Walter Horsford, shortly before his execution, placed in the hands of the Governor of Cambridge Prison a written statement confessing his guilt and admitting the justice of his sentence.

Justice Hawkins received some criticism for the case. There was an accusation made that he had shown bias in his summing up and Horsford was said to have been convicted on circumstantial evidence. In 1904 the publishers Thomas Nelson and Sons produced a book entitled *The Reminiscences of Sir Henry Hawkins, (Baron Brampton)*. In Chapter 35 Sir Henry answers the criticism that he 'had gone quite to the limits of a Judge's rights in summing up the case'. He described the detail of the case, then his summing up and the circumstantial evidence, then poses the question:

> If a Judge may not deal with the fallacies of a defence by placing before the jury the true trend of the evidence, what other business has he on the Bench? And it was for thus clearly defining the issue that someone suggested a petition for a reprieve, on the ground that the evidence was *purely circumstantial*, and that my 'summing up was *against the weight of the evidence*'. Truly a strange thing that circumstances by themselves shall have no weight.
>
> But there was another strange incident in this remarkable trial: *the jury thanked me for the pains I had taken in the case*. I told them I looked for no thanks, but was grateful, nevertheless.
>
> I have learnt that the jury, on retiring, deposited every one on a slip of paper the word 'Guilty' without any previous consultation – a sufficient indication of their opinion of the *weight* of the evidence.
>
> This was the last case of any importance which I tried on circuit, and if any trial could show the value of circumstantial evidence, it was this one. It left the identity of the prisoner and the conclusion of fact demonstrable almost to mathematical certainty.
>
> A supposed eye-witness might have said: 'I saw him write the paper, and I saw him administer the poison.' It would not have added to the weight of the evidence. The witness might have lied.

Throughout the investigation there appears to have been no mention of a young woman named Fanny James although her story appeared in the *St Neots' Advertiser* shortly after Horsford's execution in an article entitled 'Singular Co-incidence'.

When he was in his late teens Horsford had courted James and they both lived at Stow Longa. In 1890 James decided to visit her sister-in-law and went by trap to Kimbolton then by train on to Kettering.

In December, some weeks after her arrival, she received a letter. After supper she took it to her room. When her sister-in-law eventually went to say goodnight to her she found James suffering convulsions – symptoms that fitted the description of strychnine poisoning. Just before her death she cried out, calling Walter Horsford by name.

An inquest was held on the following day but concluded that James had died 'through eating a hearty supper'. Despite the misgivings of some of her relatives the police did not consider Horsford could be in any way responsible as he had been so far away in Stow Longa at the time of her death.

Interestingly she had been pregnant at the time of her death.

One of her relatives, known only as Mr James, worked for Horsford as a farm-hand. He commented to some of his co-workers that he suspected that his boss had been involved in Fanny's death.

Soon afterwards Horsford offered to buy him a drink. They visited a local pub and Horsford handed him a beer. Within minutes James was feeling ill. He hurried home but died very soon afterwards.

His death was not treated as suspicious, but after Horsford's conviction it was decided that this and other unexplained deaths should be investigated. The *Illustrated Police News* printed the stories of the deaths of both Fanny James and her relative as well as the following:

> The third case of alleged poisoning is that of a servant girl at Peterborough who was know to be intimate with Walter Horsford, who was in the habit of visiting Peterborough market. It is alleged that this girl received a packet stated to be addressed in Horsford's handwriting, and died the same night with symptoms of poisoning. It is doubtful whether the document written by Horsford and purporting to contain a confession of the crime for which he was executed last week, will ever be made public, though it is understood that Horsford's friends will shortly be supplied with a copy of it.

Despite these rumours nothing else was ever proved.

The Horsford case became the subject of at least one street ballad. One entitled *The Execution of Walter Horsford* credits him with coming from St Neots. Perhaps it would have been more fitting for him to have been known as the Spaldwick Poisoner. Equally inaccurately the ballad seems to think that Horsford deserved some sympathy. As he acted neither in the heat of the moment nor after any great provocation and was certainly one of Cambridgeshire's most cold-blooded killers, any sympathy would be misplaced.

Notes

1 Strychnine occurs naturally in a variety of seeds and plants, especially the dog button plant, indigenous to India, Hawaii and other tropical countries. The fruits resemble mandarin and the seeds are large, and a velvety looking grey. Strychnine is colourless with a bitter taste and affects the central nervous system with symptoms that are very similar to those of tetanus. Medically it was developed as a stimulant and sometimes as an ingredient in preparations for the treatment of nausea. It was used most commonly as a rat poison.

2 Dover Powders or Dover's Powder: a powdered drug containing ipecacuanha and opium, formerly used to relieve pain and induce perspiration. After Thomas Dover (1660–1742), British physician.

3 Now St Neots' Museum.

4 Palliasse: mattress consisting of a thin pad filled with straw or sawdust.

5 A drachm is a unit of apothecary weight equal to ⅛ of an ounce or to 60 grains.

6 Neuralgia is acute spasmodic pain along the course of one or more nerves.

9

AN IRONIC TWIST
OF THE KNIFE

James Henry Hancock was executed for a murder committed on the evening of 4 March 1910. Hancock was a 54-year-old labourer, who had lived with a woman named Eliza Marshall for fourteen years. She was also known as Eliza Chapman and was a married woman living apart from her husband, at 22 Water Street, Chesterton.

Mrs Marshall, four years older than Hancock, earned her living by taking on casual work at fairs, travelling with a caravan in the summer, and in wintertime hawking coke in the Cambridgeshire villages.

Hancock was known by the nickname of 'Sonny'. He had originally come from Sheffield and moved to Cambridge in the mid-1890s when the drainage work on the Fens was being carried out.

During the time that Hancock and Marshall lived together they had frequent rows and it is said that Hancock twice left and returned to Sheffield. But each time he came back to Cambridge, again to live with Marshall. Towards the end of their relationship however, Marshall tried to separate from Hancock, saying that she could not live with him any longer. She even went as far as to make a complaint to the police about him.

On 4 March Marshall and Hancock had arranged to go to Cottenham with a load of coke. At about 6 a.m. Hancock took their horse and cart and went to the gas works to pick up the load. Marshall met him there at just after 7 p.m. Hancock had loaded the cart by then and so they set off.

Shortly into the journey a quarrel broke out between them, the exact cause of which was unclear, but it was resolved with Hancock declaring that he would not go to Cottenham. Apparently Hancock wanted to sell the coke in Cambridge while Marshall wanted to adhere to the original plan and take it to Cottenham. When Hancock declined to go any further Marshall said that she would get her brother, Alfred Doggett, to go with her.

Doggett, aged about 60, lived in Red Barn Cottages in Old Chesterton. He came to meet them with a view to his taking over the cart. This possibility enraged Hancock and the two men began to argue. Hancock threatened Doggett with violence and took the horse home, to unharness it and put it in its stable.

When Marshall arrived home Hancock baldly stated that he wanted his clothes and that she would not have any more worry with him. She took this to mean that he was leaving again. Therefore she and her brother re-harnessed the horse and returned to the original plan of going to Cottenham. When they returned Doggett saw to the horse while Marshall went indoors. Hancock was still there and had made tea. He asked her to join him but she refused, being still annoyed with him. This renewed Hancock's bad temper and he slammed the door in her face.

She went across to the stable to help her brother with the horse, and after a few minutes Hancock joined them. A brief discussion ensued culminating in Hancock asking Doggett, 'Have you got over your temper?' which was met by stony silence.

What happened in the next few moments is not clear; Marshall's story differed from Hancock's. However, with or without provocation from her brother, it is clear that Hancock struck Doggett and, as she saw her brother fall to the ground, Marshall realised that Hancock held a knife in his hand.

She pulled the knife away from Hancock, suffering a minor injury to her hand, and then ran from the stable. Doggett staggered after her with blood gushing from a wound to his neck. He managed to cross the road but then fell and died almost immediately. On examination the wound was measured at almost 5in long and was deep enough to have sliced the jugular vein and damaged bone.

Hancock made no attempt to escape and when Edwin Phillips, who worked for the university, stopped to ask him what he was doing Hancock said, 'I'm sorry for what I've done but meant killing her.' He later repeated this claim to another witness when he said, 'I killed him, but I killed the wrong one.' Then, on his arrest by a policeman, Constable Lander, he shouted, 'Here you are, Mr Lander. I have done it, but it ought to have been old 'Liza and all'. On the way to the police station he added: 'I hope he's dead. I hit him hard enough anyway. I plead guilty, but I wish it had been the other old **** as well. I did try but the knife was not strong enough. I don't care. I shall get three weeks before I get my neck stretched, and then I shall have some beer.'

The following evening Hancock made a further statement to Constable Evans, which included: 'She wanted me to go to Cottenham with her, but I did not want to go. He went with her, and when they got back old 'Liza started swearing, and he started shouting. I soon stopped him and I should have soon stopped her if she had not soon got out of the way. I stopped him. I stuck the knife into him. They have always been against me. About fourteen years ago he kicked me in the jaw. She won't be able to fly to him in the future.'

At his trial on 28 May Hancock claimed to have had a legitimate reason for possessing the knife and claimed that he did not know how Doggett had been injured. He also swore that he had no recollection of the fight. Despite efforts by his counsel, Grafton Pryor, and his solicitor, G.A. Wootten, the judge, Justice Phillimore, found him guilty and passed the death sentence.

James Hancock was executed at 8 a.m. on 14 June 1910 despite about 500 signatures being obtained in an effort to obtain a reprieve. Henry Pierrepoint was the executioner and was assisted by his brother Thomas. Death was said to be instantaneous. In an ironic twist it was later discovered that Doggett had been one of the workmen who had helped to build the scaffold that was used for the execution of his murderer.

Subsequent to the report of James Hancock's execution the following interesting article appeared in the 17 June edition of the *Cambridge Independent Press*:

A CENTURY'S RECORD
Previous Executions in Cambridge.

It is 12 years since the extreme penalty of the law was last paid within the walls of the County Gaol, so that Tuesday's execution is the first that has taken place here in the 20th Century. The last culprit was Walter Horsford, the notorious St Neot's poisoner, who was hanged on the morning of Tuesday June 28th 1898 for the murder of his cousin, Mrs Holmes. Prior to that date there was a long period during which the hangman was not called upon to perform his dread office within the county, for it was as far back as December 14th 1876, that the previous execution took place – that of Robert Browning, for the murder of a woman named Emma Rolfe, on Midsummer Common.

The last public execution in the county was on March 11th 1864, when John Green was hanged for the murder of a girl at Whittlesey. Shortly after this the law was passed putting a stop to executions in public, and the tendency since then has been more and more towards complete privacy, so much so that it seems somewhat difficult now to realise that not 50 years ago an execution was the occasion for the assembly of huge crowds of people who used to regard it very much in the light of a public holiday. There are not a few still living who can remember these grim exhibitions, when people flocked into the town from many miles around to see the unhappy wretch expiate his crime on the gallows. One gentleman remembers that when a boy at school at Huntingdon the father of one of his schoolfellows came to the school to fetch his son away for the day in order to take him to Cambridge to see an execution.

These unedifying exhibitions have, happily, been abolished, and now the executions are carried out in such strict privacy that even the representatives of the Press, those indispensable watch-dogs of the public are not always allowed to be present.

A GRIM RECORD
The records of the last century show some 26 persons have suffered the death penalty in Cambridgeshire during that period. Of these, however only four were executed during the latter half of the century, and only two since public executions were abolished. In the early days of the 19th Century people were hanged for much less serious offences than that of murder. Thus the century's grim record commenced with the hanging of William Grimshaw in March 1801 for housebreaking and in April of the following year William Wright and Robin Bullock were put to death for arson. Then

came an interval of 10 years, but in 1812 there were two executions, the first being that of William Nightingale, alias Bird, on March 28th, his offence being forgery, and the second, on August 8th, that of Daniel Dawson, for poisoning a horse at Newmarket.

Four years later came the Littleport riots for taking part in which John Dennis, Isaac Harley, Thomas Smith, William Beamise and George Crow were hanged together at Ely on Friday June 28th. The offence charged against them was that of 'felony in the sad and dreadful outrages that had taken place at Littleport, Ely, and its neighbourhood during the last week in May'. John Dennis, it seems, was a publican at Littleport, and the ringleader of the gang. He was convicted on three separate indictments of having extorted money from Ely gentlemen. Harley, Smith and Crow were labourers and Beamise was a shoemaker. All appear to have gone in for robbery, and it was stated on one occasion Smith robbed a man named Josiah Dewey, of Littleport, of 100 guineas. All five were executed near the toll-gate on the Cambridge road, and it is recorded that they were preceded to the fatal spot 'by the most respectable inhabitants of Ely, carrying white wands on horseback'. An account of the execution says that 'No words can describe the awful effect of the execution, the prisoners, with the exception of Beamise, being young man in the full vigour of life. As they moved along, St Mary's bell tolled, and the unfortunate man prayed fervently aloud and uttered the most pious ejaculations.' After many expressions of penitence and exhortations to the crowd to profit by their examples, 'the caps being drawn over their faces, they were launched into eternity'.

A DESPERATE CHARACTER
The next offender to suffer death was a well known character named John Scare, who was executed in 1817 for burglary at Whittlesford. He was only 21 years of age but he appears to have been a very desperate character and to have taken to villainy at an early age, his record, from the time of his apprenticeship to Mr. Pont, a gingerbread maker of Cambridge, until he met his end, being one of petty villainy and incorrigible scoundrelism. At one time he worked at the oil mills at Whittlesford, and at that place he robbed the house of an aged fellow-workman named Edward Stone.

Scare's heartless character was exemplified by his treatment of his wife 'with whom he lived but a few days.' He took to systematic robbery and carried a loaded pistol about with him, and such was the terror which his reckless and ferocious spirit had inspired that none dared apprehend him. But his recklessness proved his undoing, for on Sunday, as he sat boldly drinking ale at a public house at Fowlmere. The parish constable, one Rickard by name, crept up behind him and seized him, while another man snatched away his pistol.

In his confession he gave an interesting account of the burglary at Whittlesford. He stated that he and two others went to the house and broke open the window, and as his companions were smaller men, he proposed that they should go in first. They however declined on the grounds that they were 'afraid of the ghost which haunted the house.' Scare thereupon thrust his head and shoulders in at the window, exclaiming 'Now Mr Devil, either you or I'. The burglars seemed to have gone pretty openly to work, for it is stated that they put a lighted candle through the window in the belief that if there was a ghost inside it would blow the candle out. Finding that the candle still burned, they entered the house, rifled it, and went off with their booty into a field, where they put down their hats and 'threw the guineas into them as long as they lasted.' One of the thieves, named Frost, appears to have been stricken with remorse or fear, and sent his share of the spoil back to the owner, on hearing of which Scare came back from London, whither he had fled, and broke into the house again to get it. Both Frost and the third man named Teversham, were reprieved, but Scare's desperate behaviour secured him for the full rigour of the law.

INTERESTING RELICS

An interesting relic of the case, a piece of panelling from the old gaol, on which was carved the words, 'C Teversham crost this bridge the last time March 14th, 1819, after 2 years' was in the possession of Mr John Whitaker, curio dealer, of Sidney Street, as was also a record of the crime of murdering his wife, for which Thomas Weems was hanged at Cambridge on August 6th 1819. This appears to be the first murder of the century so far as

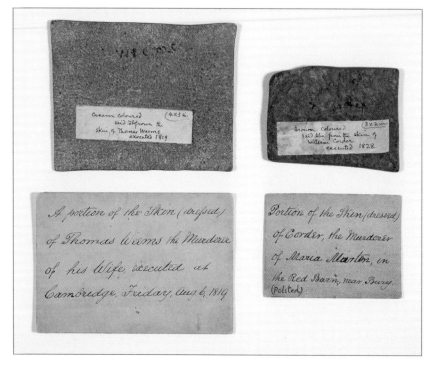

Preserved squares of skin from Corder and Weems. (Trinity College Library)

Cambridgeshire was concerned. A somewhat gruesome relic of this murder is, or was, preserved in Trinity College Library in the shape of a square piece of Weems' skin, dressed and carefully labelled and preserved. Alongside it was kept a similar piece of skin taken from the body of Corder, the notorious Red Barn murderer, whose crime near Bury St. Edmunds gave rise to so much excitement at the time, and on which a play was written which still has a vogue in travelling theatres. This fearsome relic is tanned and of considerable thickness. It is said that at Bury St Edmunds there is a book containing an account of Corder's life, covered with leather made from his skin.

DEATH FOR HIGHWAY ROBBERY

The gallow's next victim was one John Lane who on April 3rd 1824, was hanged for rape. Another five years elapsed before William Osborn was hanged for highway robbery. Osborn was a native of Boxworth, and the robbery was committed at Elsworth. The victim of the robbery was David Darwood, of Warboys, a higgler whom Osborn saw with some money at a public house in Knapwell. Osborn went out first, waylaid him on the road to Conington, called on him to deliver, and murderously assaulted him with a 'dibbing iron', afterwards robbing him of twelve sovereigns and a £5 note on the Baldock Bank. But Darwood recovered to identify his assailant, and the 'dibbing iron' covered with blood and hair, helped to seal Osborn's fate, which he met in April 1829.

The next execution took place on April 3rd, 1830, when three labourers, named Wm. Reader, Wm. Turner and David Howard, were hanged for having 'wilfully and maliciously destroyed several stacks of corn and other property belonging to Mr. Chalk, at Linton, and Mr. Sharp, of Badlingham'. The Cambridge Free Library contains an interesting account of this and other crimes.

The attempted murder of a gamekeeper three years later brought Wm. Westnot and Chas Carter to the scaffold on March 30th, 1833, and in December of the same year John Stallan was hanged for arson. For 17 years after this the gallows was not required, and then, on April 13th, 1850 Elias Lucas and Mary Reeder were executed for poisoning the former's wife at Castle Camps. The case excited tremendous interest in the county and a great crowd witnessed the execution at Cambridge. On August 10th, 1861, the gallows was again requisitioned for the punishment of Augustus Hilton for cutting his wife's throat with a razor at Parson Drove. Then, three years later, came the last public execution in Cambridgeshire, that of John Green, on March 11th, 1864. The next execution was that of Robert Browning, on December 14th, 1876, when, although the execution was carried out in private, a great number of people came into the town in the hope of seeing something of it.

The last execution, that of Walter Horsford, took place at Cambridge County Gaol on Tuesday 28 June 1898 at 8 a.m.

HUNTINGDONSHIRE CASES

The records of other Huntingdonshire cases show that at the Hunts. Assizes in July, 1827, Joshua Slade was sentenced to be hanged two days later, but was respited until September 1st, when he was hanged on Huntingdon Common, near where the gallows now stands. After the barbarous fashion of the time, the body was dissected, and the public were allowed to view the remains. Another case was that of Jas. Bishop, who was executed in 1829 for sheep stealing, the execution taking place in front of the newly erected gaol at Huntingdon. On 6 November 1878 Henry Gilbert was tried at Cambridge, before Mr Justice Hawkins, for the murder of a child at Hall Weston, and found guilty, but recommended to mercy. He was, however, executed at Huntingdon on Monday 25 November 1878 Marwood being the executioner. The last charge of murder in Hunts. prior to the case of Horsford was in November, 1883, when David Wombwell was tried at Cambridge Assizes for the murder of W.J. Snelling at the Falcon Brewery, Huntingdon, but was acquitted.

10

A GOOD NIGHT OUT AND A BAD NIGHT INN

Hotels bestowed with the name Temperance in their title were traditionally advertising themselves as teetotal establishments; the revelation that alcohol played a part in the events which occurred on Saturday 1 February 1913 added irony to the scandal.

The Temperance Hotel was owned by Elizabeth Warnes who was 46. She had been born Elizabeth Barton and had grown up in the Romsey Town area of Cambridge. With her husband, William, she had spent several years running a sweet shop before moving to St Ives to become tenants of the Cow and Hare Hotel. It was not long before their marriage deteriorated and, after a series of rows, they decided to separate. Her husband moved away but Warnes remained in St Ives and took over the Temperance Hotel in 1909.

The Temperance Hotel – an X marks the room where the bodies were discovered (bottom right). (Norris Museum, St Ives)

When her husband left, a German, Gustave Kunne, became her regular companion. At the time of his death he was aged 44. He and a fellow German, Frederick Finke, had both come from a village called Hohendodeleben, near Magdeburg, to work at Wootten and Sons' chicory factory in Fenstanton. They were employed as driers and worked at the factory's kiln. Kunne was married with four children – three girls and a boy – and when work was not busy he made visits home. In the summer of 1912 his wife had died and his children had gone to live with her sister. The last of his visits to his family had seen him arrive back in England on 12 October 1912. He had lodgings in Fenstanton but was a frequent visitor to the Temperance Hotel, often visiting both at weekends and during the week.

Lucretia Cooper was a servant of Warnes, and was known by her middle name of May. Saturday nights were her regular evenings off and she had been to the local picture palace accompanied by a St Ives man, William Walker. Walker had walked her back to the Temperance Hotel where they arrived shortly before 10 p.m. to find the hotel locked and the lights out.

At first they were not concerned; she had seen Warnes earlier in the evening in the company of Kunne and her brother-in-law, Thomas Allen. As far as Cooper had been aware the mood between the three had been good.

So she and Walker waited around for some time until eventually they decided to call upon a friend of her employer in the hope of finding her there. Having been unsuccessful it was just after half-past eleven when they returned. Only then, in an attempt to gain entry, did Cooper discover that the back door of the hotel was unlocked.

She said goodnight to her companion and made her way inside, heading straight for the ground floor tearoom, which was used by Warnes as a living room. Pushing the door she found that something was wedged against it from the inside preventing it from fully opening. She struck a match to help her see what the blockage was. To her horror she saw Kunne's apparently dead body heaped on top of the equally lifeless body of Warnes.

Cooper ran from the hotel, back into the street, where she called for help from Walker who had not gone far. He summoned assistance from the St Ives police; Inspector Gale arrived on the scene within minutes. Walker was also sent to bring Dr Grove to the hotel.

With proper lighting Gale made his initial inspection of the scene. His immediate observation was that both Warnes and Kunne had been dead for some time. He also noted that Warnes was still wearing her jacket and had a single stab wound to her chest, in the region of her heart.

Grove arrived at approximately half-past twelve. His conclusion, from the temperatures of the bodies, was that they had both been dead for almost three hours. He agreed with Gale that the woman had clearly been stabbed and, after a brief search, they found a large clasp knife near Kunne's right hand. Grove quickly came to the conclusion that Kunne had stabbed Warnes before killing himself. As Grove had seen no obvious injury to the dead man he set about

Gustave Kunne (Norris Museum, St Ives)   *Elizabeth Warnes* (Norris Museum, St Ives)

searching for a container that may have held some fast acting poison. It was only when he searched Kunne's body that he finally saw a single stab wound to the heart.

An inquest was held in the afternoon of Monday 3 February 1912 in the Magistrate's Room in St Ives. The deputy coroner, A.H. Barratt, led the proceedings with a jury consisting of G.J. Meadows (foreman), J.S. Briggs, H. Dawson, R.W. Glenn, G.H. How, A. Hurl, J. Jaffarey, G. James, F.W. Kirby, A. Nelson, A.W. Parfitt, H. Parker and W.J. Smith. Also present was Superintendent Griffin on behalf of the police.

Barratt opened the inquest by outlining the events surrounding the discovery of the bodies and the apparent cause of each death. He explained that the inquests for both deaths would be held as one and the jury would be asked to consider three possibilities; firstly whether Kunne had murdered Warnes then killed himself, secondly whether Warnes had killed Kunne before killing herself or lastly whether they had both died in a suicide pact.

The jury were taken to inspect the bodies before being transported to the Temperance Hotel to view the room in which the bodies had been found. Once they had seen the scene they returned to the Magistrate's Room.

Mrs Warnes was identified by her brother-in-law, Thomas Allen. Asked when he had last seen her alive he described the time he had spent with her on the day of the murder. He had arrived from Cambridge by train at about 2.15 p.m. and had spent the rest of the day in St Ives in her company.

At seven in the evening, or soon afterwards, they had been joined by Kunne, a man whom Allen had never before met. Kunne and Warnes seemed to be on good terms and they accompanied him to the Great Eastern Railway Station where he caught the 8.57 p.m. train back to Cambridge.

When Superintendent Griffin asked him when he last saw his sister-in-law before the day in question, Allen answered: 'I should think it would be about six months ago.' He then stated that she had never, by word or letter, ever mentioned Kunne to him. He also claimed that he was not aware of the nature of the relationship between Warnes and Kunne, nor had he been given any feeling that his presence had caused any upset.

It was Frederick Finke who identified Kunne. He explained the deceased's home life and the nature of their employment at Wootten and Sons. He also mentioned that Kunne was notoriously short tempered but, during the last three weeks of his life, had been more fractious than usual. This had made him difficult to get along with and had led Kunne to neglect his work.

The next witness was Lucretia May Cooper. She detailed her employment with Warnes, saying that she had begun working for her on 29 December 1910. According to her statement, it was after working at the Temperance Hotel for a week that she had first met Kunne.

On the night of the deaths she had departed for her evening out at seven-thirty. She described Warnes and her guests, Thomas Allen and Gustave Kunne. As far

as she knew all three of them seemed happy. She went on to describe the discovery of the bodies, mentioning that the back door must have been left unlocked by mistake. When asked whether she had actually entered the room she confirmed that she had not.

Griffin decided to change his line of questioning. He asked, 'Have you ever heard any quarrels between Mrs. Warnes and Kunne?' Cooper replied that she had heard one the previous year. When pressed as to when during the year Cooper responded that it was shortly before Kunne had returned to Germany. This dated the row to the early part of the previous summer. According to her the argument was based on jealousy.

The Temperance Hotel today. (Stewart P. Evans)

Barratt, the coroner, asked: 'Can I take it the man accused the woman of going out with another man?'

'No,' May clarified. 'She was out with another lady friend.'

Next Griffin asked whether there had been any other quarrels. At first Cooper played them down saying that there had been just little tiffs, but the coroner reminded her of a major quarrel that had taken place just before Easter of 1912. Apparently, this too had been the result of Warnes taking a walk with another woman. This quarrel had led to Kunne assaulting Warnes.

Through Cooper answering a series of questions put to her by the coroner, a picture was painted of a row which had taken place at the bottom of the stairs at the Temperance Hotel and culminated with Kunne grabbing Warnes around the waist and her struggling to get free of him. May had unsuccessfully tried to separate them and in the end the police had been called. The attending officer Constable Bailey was not called to give evidence. Cooper had seen no signs of injury to Warnes but had noted that Kunne had sported a black eye afterwards.

Although she had heard Kunne say nothing on the subject, Warnes had told her servant that he wanted her to get a divorce from her own husband so that he could marry her.

Inspector Gale took the stand and handed May the clasp knife and asked whether she was familiar with the tool. 'Yes, Sir. It belonged to Mr Kunne,' responded the witness. She agreed with Gale that Kunne had practically taken the place of master of the house and, in describing the dead man's personality, said 'Kunne would sometimes stamp his foot in a rage.' A few minutes later she added that he was very jealous of her.

The next witness called was Harry Sines who had been in the Railway Inn from about 9 p.m. Warnes and Kunne were already there, having just waved off the Cambridge train. The three of them walked towards the town centre and had something to drink in the Robin Hood public house. At half past nine they reached the Temperance Hotel and he left their company. In the time he had spent with them they had both been friendly and sober.

Gale's statement filled in more details. Warnes' body had been behind the door, face down with her head about a foot from the corner of the room. The man was lying on his left side across Warnes' waist and with his left arm through a deep hole in the lace curtains that extended to approximately two feet in length. Kunne's left hand stretched out, almost around her neck. Gale had touched their skin and found it to be slightly chilly. Warnes was still dressed for outdoors. When the inspector opened her jacket he had seen that there was obvious bleeding.

On inspecting the area around the bodies he discovered the clasp knife, a battered felt hat which looked like the one that Kunne had been wearing and a broken lamp. The glass globe and chimney of the lamp were smashed: the shards and some spilt paraffin were lying in the chair. The lamp was unlit but had been replaced in an upright position on the table. Aside from the damaged lamp and the fact that the table appeared to have moved by a few inches, the room showed no signs of disturbance.

Gale had also observed the presence of several empty beer bottles and glasses, and one almost full glass of stout.

The coroner asked Gale whether he knew either or both of the deceased. Gale replied, 'I have know the woman since I have been here, and that is five years. Three years ago Mrs Warnes' husband kept the Cow and Hare. In September 1909, they had been quarrelling and fighting and both bore marks of violence. They then parted and the husband had hardly been to St Ives since.' Gale went on to explain that he had often seen Kunne with Warnes, and that the two had been under observation since a complaint in April 1912. Then, at Easter 1912, Constable Bailey had to be called for the incident at the bottom of the stairs. Two days later Gale had observed that Kunne had two black eyes.

Dr Grove's description of the scene matched Gale's, although he added that there was blood on the knife and also on the inside of Kunne's right hand, and a little on the outside of Kunne's left hand. There was also a moderate amount of blood under the woman's body.

Grove had made the post mortem examination on Sunday 2 February. He began his testimony by describing the state of Kunne's body. The man was described as 'exceedingly fat' and his enlarged liver showed that he had been a heavy drinker. The fatal injury was a single stab wound that had passed between the ribs, piercing the heart. The blade had gone in horizontally and at almost 90° to the chest.

Although Mrs. Warnes had also died from a single stab wound to the heart her injury was somewhat different: the blade had been almost vertical when it had entered and had travelled diagonally downwards. It had entered the chest wall approximately an inch lower than it had entered the skin and had cut across the heart, leaving a large gaping wound.

In Grove's opinion both deaths would have been almost instantaneous. On both victims the wound was approximately one eighth of an inch narrower than the blade of the knife but the doctor explained that was consistent with the elasticity of skin. Also from the lack of any other disturbance in the room he strongly discounted that there had been any third party involved in the incident.

He discounted the suggestion that Warnes could have killed Kunne before killing herself, explaining that she must have died first for her body to have been found underneath. Griffin asked whether it would have been possible for the wound to be self-inflicted. Grove replied that he would expect a self-inflicted wound to go straight inwards: 'The direct wound being downwards and the cut being vertical was against it being inflicted by herself. It would be extremely improbable, so improbable as to be impossible.' He explained that the extent to which she would have needed to twist her wrist around have left her unable to exert sufficient force upon the knife to make the fatal wound.

Grove stated that he believed that only someone standing in front and above her could have inflicted Warnes' wound. That left Grove with only one conclusion: that Kunne had killed Warnes before turning the knife upon himself.

He explained the evidence by drawing the following scenario:

Mrs Warnes and Gustave Kunne had returned to the Temperance Hotel and had gone into the tearoom. Kunne had already made his plan and carried the clasp knife in readiness. Mrs Warnes had taken the seat near the window and had sipped her glass of stout. He had drunk beer, possibly to help him carry out his plan. To ensure that he took Mrs Warnes by surprise he had deliberately knocked the lamp. He returned the lamp to the table before plunging the knife into her breast. Her weight unbalanced him and he ripped through the lace curtain before falling on her.

This idea did not explain how Kunne had had sufficient light to stab Warnes accurately, or how the glass from the lamp ended up on the chair if he was sitting on it as it was broken. Neither did it explain how her weight had unbalanced the heavy man if she was still sitting or the likelihood that he had stabbed himself after falling.

Another policeman, Constable Coulson, had gone with Frederick Finke to Kunne's room where he had discovered letters from Warnes. The servant girl, Cooper, identified the handwriting as that of her employer.

The coroner adjourned the inquest for almost an hour. He used the time to look at the letters to determine whether anything contained in them would have bearing on the case. At 6.30 p.m. the inquest was re-convened and Barratt, the coroner, described the notes as affectionate. He felt it was essential for the jury to hear extracts from selected letters.

The first was dated 16 April but without a year. It was assumed that the year in question was 1912. Warnes had written: 'As soon as I got in the house why did you not tell me what you had to say and where I had been. I was not with anyone else. I went to buy Easter eggs for you to send away and that is what I got in return when I got home. I was surprised at the way you treated me. You tried to kill your Lil, that is what you always said you would do, and perhaps it is not too late. But be careful what you do; you see I shall not be afraid. I shall still hold my own.'

On 12 May she wrote: 'I am sorry we met as we did and then to end like this. You know I often told you, the reason I left "Mr W" because he did not treat me well. Then you say you love me as you do, then for you to do the same. My throat has been very bad. Lots of blood has come from it, but it is much better now. Sorry to write like this, but I never thought I could. I feel I must forget you and you must forget me as much as possible.'

Kunne received her letter of 27 June just before his trip home to Germany. This missive was clearly in reply to a communication he had made to her. In it she had written: 'When you say suicide, I hope it is not my doing'.

Further on she had said: 'Don't let things worry you too much. I shall not be able to go for my holiday yet, as I have people staying, but I feel a little better than last week. Dear G, you have asked me to forgive you, I will do so, but it is impossible for me to forget. You must not show your temper again to me.'

The final communication read was an undated letter referring to October 1912.

October will soon slip by and you will be early then. Have no fear. You say I am cruel in not writing more lovingly to you. That may be to you also my revenge. You remember, George, you had your revenge on me for nothing, and I am not man mad, and I cannot say how things will turn out for us, but whatever it may be we will have things straight.

In his summing up the coroner still directed the jury to his three original options: the man had killed the woman, the woman had killed the man, or that it was a double suicide. In contradiction to the previous statements Barratt described both the fire and lamp as still being alight. He reminded the jury that Kunne had been shown to find his temper hard to control, and that Warnes' letters had demonstrated the intense and jealous nature of their relationship. He went on to remind the jury that Grove had thought it impossible that Warnes' wounds were self-inflicted. His personal opinion was that the scenario suggested by Grove was the most probable and Kunne would have been driven by his love for Warnes.

The jury retired, but after only twelve minutes they returned with their verdict. Their conclusion was that Mr Kunne had 'intentionally and with malice' killed Warnes before killing himself. 'Had he', the coroner asked the jury, 'at the time he committed the crime, full possession of his mental faculties?'

'Yes,' replied Mr Meadows, the foreman.

A verdict of murder and felo de se[1] was recorded and the inquest was concluded at 7.25 p.m.

Warnes was buried in the afternoon of Wednesday 5 February. The cortege left from outside the Temperance Hotel at just after 2 p.m. and the Revd O.W. Wilde conducted the service in front of a packed church. At the cemetery over 200 people were present along with the family mourners who included Warnes' three brothers and one sister, their spouses and children.

The inscription on the coffin read

In loving memory of
ELIZABETH WARNES
Died February 1st 1913
Aged 46 years

Three wreaths accompanied the coffin and these read 'With deepest sympathy from brother Walter, wife and family', 'In loving memory from brother George and family' and 'In loving memory of our dear sister, from brother Harry and family'.

By contrast, at the funeral of Kunne, held the next day, only his employer, Mr Wootten and Frederick Finke, were mourners. The grave was dug in the north-east corner of the cemetery. Although a large crowd had gathered to watch the burial they remained silent throughout.

Because of the haste with which the inquest was concluded rumours persisted that the final verdict may not have been correct. These included various inaccuracies, such as reports of the lamp mysteriously being re-lit by the time the bodies were discovered.

Warnes's husband and the woman she went out with were never called to give evidence. There was no explanation as to why the rear door had been left unlocked. The evidence given was circumstantial but from the history of their relationship and the evidence pointing to Kunne's foul temper and jealousy, his actions were necessarily not out of place. But there is no doubt that the inquest could have been more thorough and had modern forensic techniques been available the conclusions drawn would have been less questionable.

There are several ways that the final moments of their lives can be pictured but it is difficult to envisage a scenario that includes the lamp being righted once the attack began. If Warnes had been stabbed while sitting, then the lamp could not have been broken beforehand as the glass was on the seat of her chair.

Notes
1 Felo de se: suicide; formerly a criminal act in the UK, but repealed in 1961.

11

EAT, DRINK AND BE MURDERED

Although the last execution of a Cambridge murderer occurred in the 1930s it was in 1913 that the last execution took place in Cambridgeshire itself. The village of Brampton is in the north of Cambridgeshire and every year held its annual feast. The festivities usually continued well into the night and, for many feast-goers, part of the attraction included the opportunity to consume plenty of alcohol.

Two of those attending the spectacle, Frederick and Martha Jane Seekings, were assumed to be man and wife. Frederick was variously reported to be between 35 and 39 years old, and originally from the Chatteris area. He was later described by the rector of Brampton, Revd Knowles, as a man with no friends and only a small intellect to whom it was necessary to speak as if to a child.

Martha meanwhile was in her mid-forties and by the standards of the day had led a wild life. After her death it transpired that she and Frederick had never been married and her correct surname was Beeby. She had been born to Thomas and Charlotte Gunn of Denford near Thrapston. Martha married Leonard Beeby and they had four children, three of whom were still alive at the time of her death. The family moved to Desborough and then Rothwell, from where, in 1894, she ran off with a showman called Blott. Leonard had not heard from his wife but thought that she had then lived with another man before Seekings.

Beeby and Seekings were together for many years, living together in Alconbury before moving to Brampton in 1906 or 1907. Also living with them was a 16-year-old lad named John Thomas Beeby who referred to them as his aunt and uncle. But he may well have been one of Martha's children.

The couple were well known for their heavy drinking. Rumours flew around the village that their excessive drinking was fuelling nasty quarrels between them. One person with a first-hand example of this was Robert Reedman who worked in the village as the chimney sweep. On asking her if she was going to the feast, Martha replied, 'Yes, I'm going if I live, and if I go there my old man says he will cut my ******* head off.' Reedman did not take the comment seriously but, when he recalled it at the inquest into her death, less than a week later, he must have wondered whether he had made a grave error of judgement.

On the feast day, Monday 28 July 1913, Seekings had been working with another labourer, Albert Wood. They had been thatching a haystack for a man by the name of Tom Stocker, the local butcher. They had worked until nearly 8 p.m. before making their way to the Bell Inn where Stocker's mother was landlady. During the day Wood saw Seekings drinking three pints of stout but was unsure how much more he had drunk between his arrival and closing time.

Shortly after eight Beeby strode into the pub and joined him. 'Oh, this is where I find you,' she exclaimed, before ordering herself a glass of beer.

By closing time (10 p.m.) there were varying reports on how much alcohol each had imbibed. Woods thought Seekings seemed sober but could not be sure about Martha. Tom Stocker, though, thought she was definitely not drunk.

In contradiction to this Edward Abrahams, who saw them outside the Bell just after ten, considered them both to be drunk. They had only just left the building when they both fell down. About five minutes later, but only ten yards further along the road, Beeby fell again, this time into a hedge. One of the staff from the Bell, known only as 'Cockney', helped to pull her up. When Seekings came up to her, they both fell into the hedge yet again.

The murder of Martha Jane Beeby. (Police Illustrated News)

Stocker had noticed that Seekings was upset. He judged the reason to be that it was because Martha had decided to attend the feast. When he saw Seekings shove her and her fall into the hedge, he intervened and offered to see them home. Stocker helped to pull her out; he took one of her arms and linked his other arm through Seekings'. They walked along the road together for a short distance before Seekings pushed her again. At this point Stocker decided to leave them to make their own way home. This was the last time she was seen alive by anyone other than Seekings.

After leaving the pub Abrahams returned home to have supper with his wife before the two of them, and their neighbour Ernest Favell, returned to the feast. The Abrahams walked around the feast field and went on the joy-wheel together before meeting up with Favell again and returning home.

They were back home shortly after eleven. When they arrived Favell's wife told them that somebody 'had been rumbling around the house' and asked them to investigate. The two men took a bicycle lamp and walked along the Thrapston Road. Within a hundred yards they saw Beeby lying on her back on the grass verge. Seekings was lying across the lower part of her body with his left arm around her legs and his right arm along the side of her body.

Abrahams called out Seekings' name several times before he moved. Abrahams shone the torch on the prone woman then bent down and touched her face; it was cold and he knew at once that she was already dead.

Favell took the lamp and waited a few yards from the body while Abrahams returned to the feast field where he found Sergeant Dighton and Constable Landin of the local police force. When the two officers arrived at the scene of the crime Seekings was initially uncooperative and addressed them with a stream of obscenities.

Dighton's view was of a woman, lying on her back, with her head towards the road. Her left leg was hooked around the right. Her dress skirt was off and lying over her shoulders, throat and face. Her petticoat was partly pulled off. The sleeve of the coat was off her right arm and her other clothing was disarranged. Her hat was on the grass on her left, about a yard away. He raised the dress skirt from her face and found her head, hair and face smothered with blood. Her throat was cut and a jagged wound ran from the right side of the wind-pipe and extended around the throat beyond the back of the left ear. The arteries appeared to be severed. There was a good deal of blood in pools on the grass and a struggle appeared to have taken place. The woman lay with her arms outstretched, and Dighton did not notice any blood on her hands. Seekings was on the left side of the woman, with his right arm under the lower part of her body. Dighton warned him that what had happened was a very serious matter and cautioned him.

Seekings replied. 'I didn't do it. She took the knife away from me and done it herself.' He then claimed that the knife was lying somewhere nearby. But after the police were unable to locate it they decided to search their prisoner. Seekings began swearing and attempted to resist but the knife was soon found in his left trouser pocket. It was a closed clasp knife that was smothered in blood. There were also bloodstains on Seekings' shirtsleeves, neckerchief, coat, arm and forearm and down the left side of his face.

The search of Seekings also revealed a pint bottle of beer and another bottle on the grass. While they waited for transport the prisoner kept swearing and asking for alcohol. Despite his unruly behaviour he was able to get into the cart without assistance and on the way to Huntingdon police station he kept repeating that he had not harmed her. He was adamant in his belief that Beeby had taken the knife away and killed herself.

Beeby's body was taken to Seekings' house where her clothes were searched. She was found to have 6d plus a few copper coins in her pockets. Dr McRitchie arrived the following morning and examined the body as it lay on a table. He determined that death had been almost instantaneous and caused by a deep 6in knife wound which had run from the right side of her neck to the left. The carotid artery had been severed and the windpipe sliced in two. Based on the position, depth and direction of the wound he concluded that it had not been self-inflicted but was the result of a murderous assault.

By the end of the week the coroner had held an inquest. He directed the jury to determine whether Seekings had murdered Beeby or if she had committed suicide. He instructed them not to consider any other possibilities. They returned eight minutes later for the foreman announced their verdict: 'the deceased met her death at the hands of Seekings while both were under the influence of drink.'

On Thursday 31 July Beeby was buried in Brampton. Two days later, on Saturday 2 August, Seekings was removed to the county gaol in Cambridge to await trial at the next assizes.

On Tuesday 14 October Seekings' trial opened with Justice Bray presiding. Beaumont Monie stood for the prosecution and Grafton Pryor for the defence.

John Beeby was the first witness called and confirmed that he had lived at Brampton for about seven years with Frederick and Martha Seekings. He had last seen Martha between 8.30 and 9.00 p.m. on the feast night and did not know if she had been drinking but had seen her drunk with Seekings on a couple of previous occasions.

Grafton Pryor asked whether Beeby had ever made any lurid claims or threats when under the influence of drink. John replied that she had threatened to kill herself, possibly by drowning. He went on to say that he had had to take a carving knife off her before because he feared that she would do something rash. Asked whether she would have gone through with committing suicide, the witness added: 'I do not think she would, because she often used to wink at me.' The latest event had occurred just the day before the feast.

Stocker was called to explain how he had helped the couple along the road, and it soon transpired that his actions had not been completely altruistic; he had wanted to make sure that Seekings would be fit to work the next day. He had been concerned that a late night at the feast would have meant that the thatching on his barn would not be completed. Stocker repeated that he did not think either Beeby or Seekings were drunk, nor had they argued, but that Seekings had seemed irritated at her presence at the fair. He probably even considered that the couple's pushing and falling over antics were more like horseplay than serious aggression. This was because the second time it happened Stocker had said: 'If you are going to act the fool, I'm off.' After which they had both walked away 'as nice as anything'.

Nothing varied in the accounts of the witnesses who had seen the couple leaving the Bell Inn or those who had discovered the body and subsequently gone for help. Favell though added that he thought Seekings had actually gone to sleep while they waited for Abrahams to return with the police officers.

A major part of the trial concentrated on trying to establish just how drunk the couple had been. The various witnesses and their definitions of drunkenness hampered this. In a rare light-hearted moment at the trial Alfred Wood, the labourer who had been working with Seekings on the day, explained that occasionally Seekings and he had drunk similar amounts: three pints during the day, then another three in the evening.

Justice Pryor asked Woods whether Seekings had been drunk. Wood explained, 'Just the same as I was. He was not drunk and he was not sober' and confirmed that meant that Seekings was capable of standing up. Pryor asked for clarification: 'And is it your view that as long as a man can stand up he is not drunk?' Wood laughed the affirmative. Bray then asked him what condition he had been in when he went to the house. Wood's response amused both the courthouse and the judge: 'As sober as a judge.'

Overall there was no consensus among the witnesses about either the amount of alcohol that Seekings had consumed or the extent to which he was inebriated. Sergeant Dighton had thought that Seekings was fairly sober: he had needed no assistance as he climbed in and out of the high trade cart that had transported him to Huntingdon police station and he had walked without staggering. In the policeman's opinion Seekings certainly had had some drink, but would have been sober enough to have known what he was doing.

Dighton was asked by the defence to consider whether the shock of finding his wife with her throat cut would have been sufficient to sober Seekings. The sergeant remained dubious; he felt that the prisoner seemed too callous to feel that shocked.

Although the doctor, McRitchie, agreed with the defence on this point he maintained that he could not envisage the fatal wound being self-inflicted.

When Seekings himself finally took the stand he admitted that he was the worse for drink 'or I should not have done such a thing, if I did do it. I don't remember doing it.'

The prosecution asked the jury to accept that the evidence showed that the wound had not been self-inflicted and that Seekings, while showing some signs of intoxication, was not so drunk that he was not aware or responsible for his actions. The defence, on the other hand, argued that in a charge of wilful murder there must be malice aforethought or premeditation, and without this the charge must be manslaughter. He asked the jury to apply the lesser charge if indeed they

The execution shed at Cambridge Gaol. (Cambridgeshire Collection, Cambridge Central Library)

did decide that Beeby had died by Seekings' hand. He asked them to consider Seekings' drunkenness as a mitigating circumstance and sought to play down claims by Stocker and Wood that Seekings appeared sober: as Stocker was the landlady's son and Wood was her employee they both had an interest in maintaining the good reputation of the pub. He also asked the jury how many sober people fell three times in quick succession.

In his summing up Justice Bray directed the jury away from the possibility that the victim had taken her own life. He said that if they concluded that Seekings was responsible that they must also consider that killing a person by cutting their throat is an effective method and therefore demonstrates the intention to kill.

On the subject of drink he added that a man might do things while drunk that he would not do when sober, but that made no difference to the outcome of the case. Only if they decided that Seekings was so drunk that he was too muddled to understand that attacking the woman with a knife was likely to cause death could they return the verdict of manslaughter.

After retiring for fifteen minutes the jury returned a verdict of guilty. Asked whether he had anything to say Seekings replied that he did not know whether he was guilty or not.

Bray placed the black cap on his head and intoned: 'The jury have found you guilty of murder. I have no choice as to the sentence I pronounce. I desire to say as little as possible on the subject. This is one of the many crimes caused by drink and the sentence of the court upon you is that you be taken from hence to the place from whence you came, and from thence to a lawful place of execution, and there be hanged by the neck until you be dead, and that your body be buried

The noose that hanged Frederick Seekings. (Stewart P. Evans)

within the precincts of the prison in which you be confined last. And may the Lord have mercy on your soul.'

On Monday 3 November 1913 Seekings was visited by his father and brother. On the following morning he was executed. Aside from his last visitors Seekings' execution attracted little interest from either his acquaintances or the public. Thomas Pierrepoint carried out the execution in the execution shed. Although a few curious people hovered around the prison gates, no bell tolled and the black flag was not hoisted. The only outward signs of the execution were the official notices posted on the gates later in the day which informed the public that the execution had gone ahead in the presence of the county under-sheriff, prison governor and the prison chaplain and that the prison surgeon, Edward Izard, had subsequently pronounced Seekings dead.

Both the rector of Brampton, the Revd Knowles, and the Earl of Sandwich had unsuccessfully written to the Home Secretary requesting that Seekings be spared the death penalty. But aside from their efforts it seems that the murder of Martha Beeby and the subsequent execution of Frederick Seekings evoked little sympathy at the time. He stands out more for his place in history as Cambridgeshire's last execution than for any criminal notoriety.

12

THE LITTLE
SHOP OF SECRETS

Cambridgeshire's most famous unsolved case is known as the Cambridge Shop Murder that occurred on 27 July in the summer of 1921. It bears marked similarities to another case, the 1919 murder of Mrs Ridgley, a shopkeeper from Hitchin. Although no conviction was made in either case the crimes were not connected.

In the 1920s King Street was narrow and busy. No. 70 was a general store selling a variety of items including tobacco, bread, cheese and margarine and was run by a spinster named Alice Maud Lawn. Miss Lawn was about 50 years old and the shop had been hers for at least twenty-one years. Although she lived alone with her cat she had relatives nearby. Her youngest brother, a motor mechanic named Horace, lived directly opposite at No. 79. She also had another brother and sister-in-law living in Cambridge.

Miss Lawn's shop was an end terraced two-storey property backing onto a green called Christ's Piece.[1] It had originally been a private house before being converted into a shop. There were two first floor bedrooms but Miss Lawn used the attic bedroom. A narrow alley called Milton Walk ran along the side of the building, with a pub called Champion of the Thames on the opposite side of this passage. There were two entrances to her property from Milton Walk; the first was a side door to the private part of the property and the second a gate to the rear garden.

Miss Alice Maud Lawn. (Cambridgeshire Collection, Cambridge Central Library)

The front of Miss Lawn's shop. (Cambridgeshire Collection, Cambridge Central Library)

Running along the back of the terrace was a public footpath that separated the gardens from the tennis courts on Christ's Piece. Miss Lawn's garden was fenced by trellis and according to the local paper it was easy to get a good view of the garden from this path. The shop was small but well stocked with one door leading from the street and a second internal door, which allowed the proprietor access to the shop from her sitting room. She seemed to live happily in King Street; she was a quiet and gentle person but popular and much respected by her neighbours.

Although Cambridge already held a market, on Market Hill, a second Wednesday market was being held in King Street. The only concern Miss Lawn seemed to have was that this market and other events attracted a large number of strangers. She was not overly confident with men and felt nervous when bands played on Christ's Piece. She told a customer: 'When the band performances are on there is such a rough crew who come here that they worry me. They rush into my shop for all sorts of things and make me very nervous indeed.'

She felt similarly worried about the Wednesday markets, which attracted strangers from as far afield as London. It was part of her routine to keep her back door locked and she would have been particularly careful on a market day. Another habit she had developed was to go out at idiosyncratic times during the day. No regular customers would have found it odd if the shop had been closed

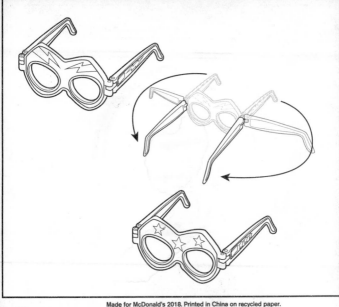

Made for McDonald's 2018. Printed in China on recycled paper.
Contents made in Vietnam in accordance with McDonald's
strict safety standards and Suppliers' Code of Conduct.
The following trademarks are owned by McDonald's Corporation and its affiliates:
McDonald's, Happy Meal, Golden Arches Logo.
HAVI Global Solutions Europe GmbH, 47059 Duisburg, Germany. © 2018 McDonald's.
JUSTICE LEAGUE ACTION: ™ & © DC Comics & WBEI. (s17)

during opening hours, they would have assumed that she had just popped out for a while. If Miss Lawn planned to go out for more than a few minutes she would tell her brother or sister-in-law living opposite.

So when, at about 11.30 a.m. on Wednesday 27 July 1921 the shop was found locked it caused no real surprise. The husband of a neighbour noticed that the shop was still locked after lunch and notified Mrs Horace Lawn. She was not aware that her sister-in-law had gone out and with some apprehension contacted her husband who was working nearby.

At about 3 p.m. Horace and his next-door neighbour, Mr Kirkup, went to investigate. They entered through the back door and immediately noticed a cupboard door open and clear signs of disturbance. Within seconds they found her body; she was lying at the foot of her stairs in a pool of blood. She had been dead for some time and had suffered a violent assault. There were savage wounds to her head and a gag hung loose around her neck.

The police were called. First on the scene was Constable Alfred Flint, an officer who had been on point duty outside a nearby post office. By the time he arrived Horace thought he had heard some noise coming from upstairs. Flint made a

Police at the crime scene in King Street. (Cambridgeshire Collection, Cambridge Central Library)

thorough search of the first floor and attic rooms but found nothing. The only thing of any note was a bowl in the scullery sink that contained water, dyed a colour consistent with blood being washed from something. A nearby tea cloth was also marked with similarly coloured smears.

The borough coroner, Mr G.A. Wootten, opened the inquest on 29 July at the Guildhall in Cambridge. After hearing the basic details of the case and hearing Horace Lawn identify his sister's body the inquest was immediately adjourned for ten days.

At this stage the police were not prepared to comment on their lines of enquiry. They had made no arrest and none looked imminent although popular opinion was that an outsider must have committed the crime. A local reporter clearly supported this view and went as far as to state: 'The police are satisfied that the murder was not the work of a local man. Jews and foreigners frequent the town, and it is possible that the man for whom the police are searching was one of the market day crowd of strangers. If the crime had been premeditated then the assailant had evidently waited for market day, when, owing to the noise in the street, any cry his victim might have uttered would have been drowned.'

The Cambridge police were quick to call for assistance from Scotland Yard; two CID officers arrived on the evening of the murder.

In the days after her death two theories were discussed, the first was that the killer had gone to the shop, posing as a customer, and had asked for something that would have required Miss Lawn to go through to her sitting room. While she was out of sight the outside door could then be locked before she was followed. The second theory was that the killer had gained access through the rear of the property and hidden there until he had had the opportunity to attack.

Meanwhile, on Saturday 30 July 1921 Miss Lawn's funeral took place at the cemetery in Cambridge's Mill Road. *The Cambridge Chronicle* and *University Journal* estimated that 1,000 people attended; the family mourners were her

Funeral carriages in King Street, Cambridge. (Cambridgeshire Collection, Cambridge Central Library)

A scene from Miss Lawn's funeral. (Cambridgeshire Collection, Cambridge Central Library)

sisters, Mrs Lincoln from Great Yarmouth and Mrs Charlton from Hendon, and her two brothers, Ernest and Horace Lawn, and their wives.

On Friday 5 August a man calling himself Jack Varden handed himself into Tottenham Court Road Police Station and claimed he was the Cambridge Murderer. He signed a statement and was then interviewed by Chief Inspector Mercer who immediately realised that the confession was a hoax. It was apparent that Varden had never even been to Cambridge. He later retracted his statement, claiming he was really called Ernest Shaw Watson and had just needed food and shelter.

When the inquest reopened on Monday 8 August the coroner first asked for post-mortem details. Dr Henry Buckley Roderick, the police surgeon, described the injuries to Miss Lawn's body: 'On examination – of course the woman was quite dead – I could see a wound on the forehead extending from the inner side of the left eyebrow upwards to the right. It was two inches long and reached down to the bone.

Her hair was matted with blood and there was obviously – although I did not examine the body at the time – a number of wounds to the scalp. The exposed parts were quite cold and as there were no signs of rigor mortis I should say she had been dead something under four or five hours.

Her head was on the mat and on the first step there was a considerable amount of blood and some had trickled down to the corner formed by the doorway into the angle at the foot of the stairs. There was of course blood on the mat and underneath the head as well – a considerable amount.'

At that point he had neither looked for nor seen a likely murder weapon and he next arranged for the body to be removed to the mortuary. It was on the following morning that he performed the post mortem. He reported:

In addition to the wound on the forehead there was another star-shaped wound about an inch above that, in the middle line of the top of the head. There were also several other wounds on the right side of the parietal[2] region, as if several blows had been struck. All of these were down to the bone, and must have been caused by considerable violence. Under one of the wounds there was an obvious depression of the skull, as though the bone had been broken, smashed in by some instrument.

The wounds must have been caused by some blunted instrument. There were other wounds further back and contusions of the left hand.

The coroner asked whether, in Roderick's opinion, the blow to the forehead was the first struck to which the doctor replied, 'from its appearance I should say it was.' But despite this he did not think it was the cause of death:

> . . . it did not crack the skull. But on further examination of the skull I found a depressed fracture extending deeply into the cavity of the skull. There was a considerable depression on the side of the fracture. The first blow would have stunned her but the second one wound have stunned her a good deal more.
>
> I should think after the first blow she was stunned – it was not an absolutely knock out blow, but stunned her for a time, and she came round, or would have come round, I should say – and then the subsequent blows were given. There was an interval between them.
>
> She could have moaned – it was quite possible. The other blows were all made about the same time (as one another), several of them at the back. After the second and the blows at the back she would not have moaned.
>
> Her eye suffered a light hemorrhage. It was of no importance.
>
> I removed the gag and examined the mouth. The gag had been forced into the mouth very forcibly, so much so that it broke one of the teeth – a molar tooth – not a very strong one – smashed it off at the base and pushed the denture forward in front of the gag. Some of the lower teeth had been loosened and the tongue had been torn, lacerated, probably by the teeth.
>
> All the internal organs were healthy, the heart and lungs showed no evidence of death by suffocation. The cause of death was hemorrhage to the brain.

Wootten, the coroner, asked whether Roderick had been shown a small chopper. Roderick replied that he had and their exchange continued with Wootten asking, 'Do you think the chopper could have inflicted the wound you have described?'

The doctor responded: 'Yes, because the back of the chopper would have given the long wound on the forehead and the others on the skull. The same instrument could have done both injuries.'

The chopper had been discovered on the day after the murder in the cupboard under the scullery sink. It had had a damp patch on it. The back of the chopper exactly fitted the large wound on Miss Lawn's forehead. Although Roderick had given his estimate of the time of death the coroner was keen to call other witnesses to help to establish a more precise time.

A baker named Albert Ding was making deliveries and one of his drops was to Miss Lawn. He had left the bakery at 10.20 a.m. and estimated that he would have been at the shop by 11.45 a.m. She had ordered a dozen 2lb loaves and paid him 6s with money from the till. He had delivered to her on numerous other occasions and knew that if she had needed to pay him a larger amount she would have gone into the back kitchen where she obviously kept more cash.

Another witness to confirm when Miss Lawn had still been alive was Mrs Ada Webb who had sent her two daughters to the shop with half a crown to buy soap and blue. The girls had left her at 11 a.m. and returned twenty minutes later with the items. The elder of Webb's daughters, Elizabeth, had said that they had been the only customers in the shop.

At 11.05 a.m. a telephonist named Arthur Sexton went to the shop to buy cigarettes and found the shop door locked. He timed his visit by the passing of the Newmarket Road bus. Although the timing of the Webb girls' visit was also approximate, they must have missed each other by only a short time.

Rose Rolph gave the next evidence. At 11.30 a.m. she cut through Milton Walk when she noticed a small sound: 'I heard a little muffled noise of some description – a sort of dull noise. I thought it was a child crying. It was a quiet noise.' She admitted that she was not sure that the noise was being made by a person but was nevertheless drawn to the sound. This evidence tied in with the account a 13-year-old named Jack Cornwell gave to the police. He had seen someone go through Miss Lawn's back gate at some time between eleven and twelve o'clock

The back of Miss Lawn's shop. (Cambridgeshire Collection, Cambridge Central Library)

A witness at the Clanwaring trial, scout John Cornwell. (Cambridgeshire Collection, Cambridge Central Library)

and had run to the gate hoping to ask for the return of a ball that he had lost in the garden a few days earlier. By the time he had reached the gate it was re-locked.

Miss Lawn's best friend, Elizabeth Papworth, described her as someone who would talk freely to customers but be guarded in relation to her private affairs. She was shown the chopper but was unable to identify it. Other witnesses who knew Alice Lawn well were also unable to recognise it, but the police eventually found proof that it was the same or similar to one Miss Lawn had kept on a table next to her scullery. The inquest was then adjourned leaving the police to ponder two possible leads.

Firstly, a young man named Leonard Marshall, an under gardener on Christ's Piece, had seen a man standing near the shop. It was between 2.30 and 3 o'clock and Leonard thought he would ask the correct time. As he approached the man he realised that he was counting some coins and decided not to interrupt him. He described the man as well dressed, wearing a light grey suit with a trilby hat. The man was of Jewish appearance and biggish built with a dark complexion. Leonard recognised the man as someone he had seen before but only on market days.

Secondly, and in seeming contrast to her private nature and her brother's observation that 'she was always nervous of any man', it transpired that she had had a lodger. The man was called Mr Grundy and had lived at the house for almost two years. He, however, had left two years previously. He had been a clerk at the Correspondence College and had suffered a mental breakdown, leaving 70 King Street after being admitted to the Fulbourn asylum. He had since been discharged from there and, as far has anyone was aware, had had no further contact with Miss Lawn.

While the second line of enquiry proved to be a dead end, Leonard's sighting of a man with a dark complexion gave the public something to focus on.

The inquest re-opened at 10.30 a.m. on Friday 19 August. The following Wednesday's edition of the weekly paper, *The Cambridge Chronicle*, blared the headlines 'WILFUL MURDER!' and 'GUARDED MAN IN COURT'. The paper gave not only the verdict of the inquest, but also the details of the arrest and committal of the new name in the case: Thomas Clanwaring.

Clanwaring was 23 and claimed that he had come to Cambridge to look for work as a French polisher. In fact Clanwaring was in such a habit of inventing stories that it soon became evident that it was almost impossible to tell when he was telling the truth and when he was just amusing himself or seeking attention.

He made several statements to the police, and in the first of these he claimed the following:

My home address is 66 New Street, Silvertown. I was born at Bethnal Green, then moved to Silvertown and have lived there ever since. I came from Baldock to Cambridge on Friday night. I have been in the town just over a week. I stayed at the Black Bull, Baldock; was there for four days. I came from Manchester to there. I had come through Manchester; I walked from Manchester to Baldock. I did not sleep a night in Manchester. From Manchester to Baldock is, I think, about 400 miles. I slept at nights under stacks. I have been from Silvertown over 3½ years. During that time I have been working for chaps on the road, shovelling up and sweeping. I came to Cambridge trying to get work as a French polisher. I tried for work at Leavis' and other places. I have only been with two chaps on two occasions since I have been in this town. Twice I have been with the two, making three persons, otherwise I have always been by myself. I can show you where one lives. Once when I was with them, the two chaps and I

Thomas Clanwaring.
(Cambridgeshire Collection, Cambridge Central Library)

went into a public house in this road where it said Under New Management. I don't know where I was on Wednesday. I know where I was on Saturday; I was in the town selling postcards.

The two chaps he referred to were Albert Briggs and Frank Turner who were also out of work labourers. This part of his statement was reasonably accurate, but virtually nothing else was; Clanwaring had been in Bedford gaol until 16 July when he had been released with the sum of 7s 6d. He had been in prison charged with the theft of five bicycles.

He had been in Bedford for five days but had no luck finding work and soon his money had run out. He went to Baldock and pretended to be deaf and dumb for three days, then went to Letchworth Baths and proclaimed: 'Oh God! Ain't it rotten.' He then told anyone who would listen that he had miraculously recovered his speech after 4½ years. He took this story to the *Daily Sketch* and hoped he would get paid for it. Part of this story was that he had originally lost his speech and hearing after the Silvertown explosion[3] and therefore gave his address as 66 New Street, Silvertown. It transpired that this was an address he had invented and he really had no home in England. When questioned in court he denied telling people he was Jewish and said, 'I don't know whether I am a Hottentot;[4] my mother was a North American and my father a South African'. When Clanwaring arrived in Cambridge he carried on telling the same deaf and dumb story and, even on the morning of Alice Lawn's murder, had been attempting to con *The Cambridge Chronicle* with it.

Clanwaring made a long statement at the inquest and was followed by Inspector Mercer who gave a detailed account of all the various and inconsistent

THE KING *v.* Thomas Clanwaring

PRESENTMENT OF THE GRAND JURY :—

Thomas Clanwaring is/are } charged with the following Offence :—

Statement of Offence :— Murder

Particulars of Offence :— Thomas Clanwaring on the 27th day of July 1921 at the Borough of Cambridge in the county of Cambridge murdered Alice Maud Lawn

Clanwaring's Statement of Offence document from the Assizes. (Author's Collection)

Clanwaring in court. (Cambridgeshire Collection, Cambridge Central Library)

statements that Clanwaring had made since his arrest. Other witnesses were called, many establishing the probable time of Miss Lawn's death and others pinpointing Clanwaring at various locations throughout the Wednesday of the murder.

The coroner warned that, of the total evidence given, only a proportion could be relied upon at a trial and that the case against Clanwaring was circumstantial. The inquest jury retired for twenty minutes and returned the verdict that they were unanimously agreed that Alice Lawn had met her death by wilful murder and that they were convinced that Thomas Clanwaring was guilty of the crime. Clanwaring was therefore committed for trial at the next assizes and held at Bedford gaol.

The trial opened on 17 October 1921 before Justice Bailhache. H.O. Carter, a London lawyer hired by a woman described only as 'a wealthy North Country lady', defended Clanwaring. She had felt moved by Clanwaring's predicament and was keen to ensure that he had the chance of a fair trial.

Full details of the crime were presented including details of Miss Lawn's financial circumstances. Based on the transactions that Miss Lawn had made during the morning of 27 July the police knew that at least a 10s note, a shilling and half a crown had been removed from the till. During the search of her house £130 had been found in notes under her carpets and lino and under her piano. In the attic they found a tin containing £13 10s in notes, £4 in silver and an old purse containing £21 in gold. There was also a post office savings book showing a balance of £469 9s 9d, making her a secretly wealthy woman. Not even her closest friend, Elizabeth Papworth and her family, knew anything about her money.

Curtis Bennett K.C. and Travers Humphreys represented the case for the Crown. The prosecution intended to call in excess of forty witnesses: they aimed to establish that it was physically possible for Thomas Clanwaring to have been at Miss Lawn's shop at the time of her death and that robbery could have been a motive. They also sought to show that Clanwaring had behaved suspiciously after Miss Lawn's death, that he had implicated himself in the murder by comments he had made, and had, according to two fellow Bedford gaol prisoners, confessed to the crime.

With this in mind Bennett showed that on the day of the murder Clanwaring had been to the mayor at 10 a.m. to obtain a pedlar's licence. At between 10.20 and 10.30 he had spoken to two women in King Street. They had stood almost opposite Miss Lawn's shop as Clanwaring had told them that he needed 25s to get photographs taken. Shortly after this he met up with Briggs and Turner, visited two local businesses and by 10.55 a.m. had entered the Rose and Crown public house in Newmarket Road where he stopped long enough to have a drink. While he was in the pub he attempted to sell a wristwatch for 4s and had apparently said: 'I would not sell this for 4s, but I'm absolutely on the rocks.' The previous evening he had also attempted to sell his cap for 1s.

Witnesses reported that he had left the pub again just before eleven. In theory he had just about enough time to have reach King Street and lock himself inside the shop before Arthur Sexton found the door locked at about five past. Clanwaring was next sighted between 11.30 and noon near 70 King Street and the Wednesday market. At 12 o'clock he entered Warrington's butcher's shop in Magdalene Street where he exchanged 10s of coppers and silver and a 10s note for a £1 note.

Next, at about 1 p.m., he went to Briggs' house and asked to swap coats. Clanwaring said he wanted to be smart for a trip to the cinema and paid Briggs 1s for the exchange. When his original coat was later examined it was stained with paint but no blood. According to the police surgeon the lack of blood did not prove Clanwaring's innocence, as the killer could have remained blood free.

At 1.30 p.m. Clanwaring returned to his lodgings, which were almost a mile from 70 King Street. He left immediately and returned between 3.20 and 3.30. By the time he came back he had purchased a stock of postcards and told his landlady that an old woman had been murdered. Miss Lawn's body had been discovered at 3.15 and the police informed at 3.25: the prosecution argued that Clanwaring had somehow heard of the murder before everybody else in Cambridge.

A number of blue Lloyds Bank bags had been found in Miss Lawn's shop and an identical one had been found in Clanwaring's possession. Firstly Clanwaring had claimed that he had found it in the street, then changed his story to say that he had taken it from the owner of a street organ when they had both been at the Racehorse pub.

How Clanwaring had gone from being penniless at just before eleven to having over a pound by lunchtime was a mystery. The coincidence of the bank bag, the change of clothes and his presence in King Street were all against him.

In addition Clanwaring was in the habit of talking to anyone prepared to listen to him and once in custody had made comments to fellow prisoners, Glenister, Bingham and Clark, that were described as 'tantamount to a confession'. On 6 August Clanwaring had said: 'I'm for it', and put his hands around his throat. 'For a watch?' Glenister asked. Clanwaring had answered: 'No, Lawn's job at Cambridge.'

On 20 August Clark testified that Clanwaring had told him: 'I shall get hung for this, but I have got the 'tecs set, as there was nobody else there but me.'

Commenting on his conversation with Clark, Clanwaring said that he had not meant to imply that he had 'done it' but simply that he would hang if he were found guilty. But all Clanwaring's denials and claims were met with scepticism and even his own defence described him as 'The biggest liar I have ever met'.

It took one hour and fifty minutes for Clanwaring to give his evidence. He swore that he had changed coats with Briggs but claimed it had been on the day before the murder. He admitted telling a Mrs Ward that someone had given him £1 but claimed that he had lied.

It was then pointed out to Clanwaring that there was a discrepancy in his evidence. In response he told the judge: 'Your lordship, I am not a very intelligent man, and I hope you will excuse me saying such a thing, but I can't penetrate my mind on these actions definitely.'

Clanwaring claimed to have raised money by starting to sell postcards almost immediately after receiving his licence from the mayor. The defence offered no proof of how he had come by enough money to buy his first stock of cards, or of exactly how he had accumulated the money in his possession.

One of the witnesses called by the defence was the Rose and Crown's barmaid, Edith Rayner, who swore that Clanwaring had been in the pub later than previously testified. She claimed it was between 11.00 and 11.30 a.m., during which time he had bought ale and tried to sell a watch. If true this would have made it impossible for Clanwaring to have locked himself in Miss Lawn's shop by ten past eleven. Her story was partially corroborated by barman Harry Farrington who had left at 10.55. Clanwaring had not arrived by this time.

The final day of the case was 20 October. Both the prosecution and defence had concluded their arguments and in his summing up the judge asked the jury to concentrate on whether Clanwaring could have been, at the very latest, inside Miss Lawn's shop at ten past eleven. If he could not have been then Clanwaring was not guilty. He directed them: 'if they thought he could have been there, this did not prove him guilty of the murder, but the Crown had got so far as "here was a man who, so far as his movements are concerned, might have committed the murder." But in this he was only one of hundreds, and before they could even then fix him with the guilt they must consider the rest of the circumstances on which the prosecution relied.'

Referring to the statement that placed Clanwaring outside Miss Lawn's shop between 11.30 and midday the judge asked how likely it was that the murderer would have loitered close by straight after committing the crime. The judge also

Left: *Clanwaring found 'Not Guilty'.* (Cambridgeshire Collection, Cambridge Central Library)

Opposite: *The Cambridge murder mystery.* (Police Illustrated News)

pointed out that there could be a reasonable explanation for Clanwaring knowing of the murder so soon. And it would have certainly been foolish for Clanwaring to announce that a murder had been committed unless he also knew that the crime had been discovered.

On the statements given by the fellow prisoners from Bedford gaol he reminded the jury that the prisoner had been 'among men whose moral values are upside down' adding 'and you have got to consider, even if these words were said whether this man then, for the first time in his life, was telling the truth, or whether he was bragging and seeking some notoriety'.

It was clear from the judge's summing up that he felt that Clanwaring should be found not guilty. The jury of eleven men and one woman returned after an hour and thirty-three minutes and at 1.20 p.m. announced that Clanwaring was a free man, to which the judge commented that he was surprised that they had not reached that conclusion sooner. Clanwaring left immediately in the company of his counsel and was reported to have been offered a job as a commissionaire at a picture palace near Leicester Square.

Based on the evidence presented in court the verdict was no doubt correct, especially as it included nothing to link Clanwaring to the crime scene. By the following week the press were already stating that they expected the crime to remain unsolved, implying that either the guilty man had been cleared or that they knew there were no further leads.

No other person was ever charged with Miss Lawn's murder. But many questions were left unanswered. Was there one killer or two? It seems reasonable to think that the killer locked the door and took money from the till but why not search the rest of the house? Did something disturb them, and if so, what?

No. 70 King Street still exists but is now a fast food shop and the building has been extended at the rear so that neither the back nor the front bears much

SCENE OF THE MURDER.

THE MURDERED WOMAN MISS LAWN

MR LAWN WHO DISCOVERED THE VICTIM

JACK CORNWELL AN IMPORTANT WITNESS

THE UNFORTUNATE WOMAN WAS FOUND WITH HER HEAD BATTERED AND HER MOUTH GAGGED.

resemblance to the shop as it would have been in 1921. However, Milton Walk and the Champion of the Thames pub still exist and the overwhelming feature of King Street is the tiny area into which the buildings are packed. Even the houses opposite are only a few feet away. It is hard to imagine that anyone thought they would be able both to enter and leave the shop without being seen.

If the killer was not an opportunist thief who managed to let a till robbery get horrendously out of hand then what was the real motive for the murder? Miss Lawn had a lot of money hidden in the house and in her post office account but had made no will. According to all those who knew her she was a sweet lady with no enemies. But in spite of this she became the victim in Cambridge's most notorious unsolved pre-war murder case and 70 King Street remains the little shop of secrets.

Notes
1 Christ's Piece was known at the time as Christ's Pieces.
2 Parietal: of or forming the walls of a body cavity, in this case the skull.
3 On 19 January 1917 a fire at a munitions factory ignited 50 tons of TNT, resulting in the largest explosion ever to occur near London. Heard as far afield as Norwich and Southampton, the explosion caused the deaths of seventy-three people and damaged over 60,000 properties. The press announcement read: 'The Ministry of Munitions regrets to announce that an explosion occurred last evening at a munitions factory in the vicinity of London. It is feared that the explosion was attended by considerable loss of life and damage to property.'
4 Hottentot: a race of people indigenous to South Africa.

13

A DIFFERENT SORT OF FIRST FOR CAMBRIDGE

Douglas Newton Potts lived in Sevenoaks, Kent. He was a brilliant student who had received a scholarship from Lancing and was studying for the Bar. He had arrived at King's College, Cambridge in October 1929. His father was picking up his college bills and, in addition to this, his scholarship was worth £80 per year.

Although he initially showed promise by the end of the first term he admitted to his father that he had slightly overspent. He had also attracted attention; neither college staff or students seemed to warm to him and felt that he seemed highly strung and slightly affected in both his manner and his dress.

One of the few friendships he managed to forge was with another undergraduate, John Frederick Gerald Newman. Potts was a talented musician and together they formed a dance band that they called the Blue Melodians, in which Potts played drums and piano and sometimes conducted.

Rather than rein in his behaviour, Potts became more eccentric. On 24 May 1930 he and Newman disappeared from college without leave. After a ten-day odyssey they returned to King's where they went in separate directions, each planning to face their respective tutors. Within a short time, shots rang out. College porters rushed to the scene only to find Potts and his tutor dead and a police sergeant mortally wounded.

The Cambridge town and the university communities were understandably shocked by the tragedy. The following day's edition of *The Cambridge Chronicle* printed photographs of the dead tutor, A.F.R. Wollaston, and the wounded policeman, Sergeant F.J. Willis. A third photograph showed King's College with its flag flying at half-mast. The public would have to wait until the inquest for further details of the murders but the account included this short obituary for Wollaston:

The death of Mr Alexander Frederick Richmond Wollaston is the severest blow to King's College. 'He was,' said the Reverend Eric Milner-White, Dean of King's, 'a most delightfully kind person. He was very popular with all sections of the university. Undergraduates were devoted to him and there was not a member of the High Table in any college who received more invitations to dine out. He had a charming wife and two delightful children to whom he was devoted. Mrs Wollaston was in London, away from Cambridge for the day. He had been tutor for two years and the ability he showed in taking over his complicated duties astonished all of us.'

He [Wollaston] was admitted to the college in 1893 and he trained for the medical profession at London Hospital. He was elected a Fellow of King's College in 1920. Distinguished as medical man, zoologist and botanist, he was a great traveller. He travelled as medical officer and naturalist on expeditions to central Africa and Dutch New Guinea during the years 1905–13. During the war he served as Surgeon-Lieutenant in the Royal Navy and he was decorated with the Distinguished Service Cross and was mentioned twice in dispatches. He received the Gill Memorial of the Royal Geographical Society in 1914 and the Patrons' Gold Medal in 1925. He was re-elected Fellow and appointed Tutor of King's College in 1928. He accompanied the first Mount Everest expedition of 1921. A native of Gloucestershire he had a home in that county. His marriage to Miss Mary Meinertzhagen took place in the College Chapel in 1929.

On the condition of Sergeant Willis the paper wrote: 'Examination of the police officer showed that he was not so seriously hurt as was at first feared, and it is expected that he will make complete recovery from his wounds.' Sadly this was not the case; Willis was weak but conscious and managed to make a statement to

Left: *Sergeant Francis James Willis.*
Above: *Mr Alexander Frederick Richmond Wollaston.* (Both pictures Cambridgeshire Collection, Cambridge Central Library)

Chief Inspector Bellamy but, later on the evening of 3 June, his condition deteriorated. He was rushed into surgery but never regained consciousness and died the following day.

A report of the incident appeared in the London press on the evening of the shooting, attracting the attention of a Miss Madge Miller, one of the few people who could shed some light on Potts and his behaviour in the days leading up to the deaths. She was among the witnesses called to the inquest on Friday 6 June, which was held in the Borough Police Court.

On the day of the shooting Wollaston had met 19-year-old Potts in Cambridge and the two of them had gone to the tutor's rooms at the ground floor of E staircase in the Gibbs Buildings in King's College. Wollaston had two rooms; the larger was accessible from the hall and led through to the smaller room where Potts and Wollaston met. The second room looked out across the lawns to the River Cam.

Sergeant Willis arrived at 1.30 p.m. with a warrant for Potts's arrest and the Head Porter, Frederick Nightingale, showed him through to the inner room. According to Nightingale, Wollaston had stood with his back to the fireplace with Potts standing near to him. The porter had left them and the only eyewitness account of what followed was in the statement made by Willis:

> I saw him outside Fitzwilliam House. I went to King's and enquired of Mr Nightingale. I went to the door and saw Mr Wollaston, and showed him the warrant, and he said you had better come in and see him. I went into the room, and Mr Wollaston came in after me. Mr Wollaston was standing with his back to the fireplace. I cautioned him, and began reading the warrant, and said, 'You will have to come to the police station.' He whipped out his revolver and fired at me. I pushed Mr Wollaston out of the way. I tried to protect him. He fired at Mr Wollaston and I tried to get at him. I fell over a chair backwards. Another bullet hit me in the left thigh. Mr Wollaston was on the ground behind me. I knew only four shots had been fired, and I thought he had another one for me, so I lay on the ground and kept still, and gradually I turned round and got up.

Willis did not mention the fifth shot. When it came it was in a final act of desperation as Potts turned the gun on himself and pulled the trigger. He did not die immediately but fell to the ground with serious head injuries. Willis struggled to the door and put up his hand shouting, 'Help, help.' Mr Nightingale ran across to find Willis sinking onto the doorstep groaning: 'He has shot me, and I shall be dead in ten minutes.'

Police and an ambulance were called, and Constable Brooks accompanied the police ambulance to King's College. The first victim he saw was Willis lying at the top of some steps. Willis told him that he had been shot in the shoulder and the lower body and that Wollaston and Potts had both also been shot. 'They are both dead,' he said. 'Look after me.'

Willis was taken to Addenbrookes Hospital (then situated opposite the Fitzwilliam Museum in Trumpington Road), and Potts followed. Dr F.B. Parsons examined Wollaston at the scene. He was lying face down and about six feet away from the dying Potts. As Parsons gently turned him over, Wollaston died. The doctor examined the tutor and found that the cause of death was a bullet wound to the chest that had gone through the sternum and embedded itself in his spine. A later examination showed that he had two more bullet wounds, one on the left side of the chest behind the arms and located near the seventh rib and the other on the top of the shoulder.

Dr James McNeil was present when Potts was admitted to hospital at 2 p.m. Potts was 'profoundly unconscious' and died at 6 p.m. The cause of death was 'laceration of the brain from a gunshot wound'.

The first wound Willis had suffered had been the one to his shoulder; the bullet had entered his upper back and exited at the front. The blood loss was small and the doctor concluded that no major vessels had been damaged. But the shot had felled Willis and, while he was on the ground, Potts had fired again. This second bullet had entered the rear of his upper thigh. There was no exit wound because it had travelled upwards into Willis's body causing extensive internal injuries. He died around 5.30 a.m. on 4 June and Dr Henry Buckley Roderick recorded the cause of death to be 'shock resulting from a gunshot wound in the perineum'.

Douglas Newton Potts. (Cambridgeshire Collection, Cambridge Central Library.

The inquest heard from a series of witnesses in an attempt to build a picture of the preceding weeks' events, which had culminated in these deaths. One of the first called was Walter Potts, Douglas's father. He had identified his son's body and explained that they had last seen each other on 22 April as his son left to return to Cambridge after visiting for Easter. Mr Potts admitted that his son 'was of a rather excitable and nervous disposition. He was highly strung.' But he also explained that he and his son had been on the best of terms and he had always had considerable confidence in him, as he had 'never caused him a moment's anxiety or worry'. Douglas's father had not suspected a problem until Monday 26 May when a letter had arrived from Wollaston explaining that Douglas had been absent for two nights.

Potts replied by sending his son a letter and a telegram asking him to get in touch and explain his absence before he had to reply to his tutor. The letter was returned. Mr Potts did not hear from his son again.

As he finished giving his evidence he said: 'May I express regret at this terrible tragedy, and at the same time, on behalf of my family say we strongly resent the newspapers' lack of humanity to those who are left behind.' This was no doubt referring to the article in the late edition of *The Times*, which came out before there had been an opportunity to inform relatives. Particularly objectionable was the portion that read: 'After shooting the two men Potts shot himself through the head. He was not killed at once, but died of his injuries in hospital this evening.'

Some of the other witnesses were other undergraduates. According to F. Clifford, a fellow member of the Blue Melodians, Potts had a 'bizarre taste in dress' and 'he used to wear grey flannel plus fours, brilliantly coloured stockings, white shoes with brown leather facings, and a high-necked jumper, either scarlet or canary yellow'. According to other descriptions he often also sported a false moustache.

One of the places Potts, Newton and some of their fellow students would visit was The Bell Hotel in the High Street , Mildenhall. This was a trip of about twenty miles and the friends would travel there in a borrowed car. The landlord's daughter commented that Potts always had 'plenty of money to spend' and never seemed to visit Mildenhall in the same car twice. He regaled locals with stories about being a prince and claimed that some of his companions were also blue-blooded.

At one point Potts had suggested to Newton that they should take to a life of crime. On occasion Potts used the *nom-de-plume* of Victor Morrell. Newton had an alias of Gordon Frazer that he never used. In fact at the inquest Newton described most of Potts' antics as 'ragging' but it seems that Potts was finding it hard to distinguish between fact and fiction. The fact that Newton went along with Potts' escapades and did not think that some of the more extreme facets of his friend's behaviour were particularly theatrical could have encouraged Potts to continue along his fantasist route.

On the evening of 4 May Potts stole an automatic pistol from another student. This may have been meant just as a prop for his fictional charades but it was not long before he drew attention to himself; Potts had visited several local gents' outfitters and at each said that he had wanted to order a suit for his friend. While this friend was being measured Potts would select other items for himself and asked to be sent a single bill to his home address. At one shop the owner refused and Potts pulled out the loaded gun and began waving it around.

The owner of the pistol, a Webley automatic, was David Gattiker. He had a firearms licence and had bought the gun and 500 rounds of ammunition from Messrs Gallyon of Bridge Street, Cambridge. He used the pistol for target practice at a local range and had last seen it on Sunday 4 May. When he went to get it the next day it had gone and he reported its loss to the police on 7 May. He knew Potts but they were not close friends.

Potts had arrived uninvited to Gattiker's rooms at about half past nine in the evening. With him were seven or eight other undergraduates. They had attended a party and were mostly acting as if they were drunk. Gattiker told Potts that he was unhappy about their presence. As far as he knew Potts had not been aware that he owned a gun but it had disappeared by the following morning.

The longest statement was made by John Newman. He had met Potts two or three weeks after arriving at King's College and they had soon become firm friends. Newman played the trumpet and they had a shared interest in music and soon formed their band.

While their friendship was still relatively new Potts had made his suggestion that they should try a life of crime. At this point Newman claimed that he found Potts to be normal but of 'a rather theatrical nature'. Therefore he did not take much notice as the suggestion had been made in front of others and was just taken as a joke.

Newman had been with Potts when he had said he was going to look up a friend and had visited Gattiker's rooms. Gattiker was out and Newman thought that Potts had left a note. While he was there Newman had noticed a gun on the top of a cupboard. Potts picked it up and took it away with him. Newman claimed he that was not sure whether his friend was borrowing it or already owned it, but admitted that Potts had later told him that the gun did not belong to him. Newman also saw the pistol on a police list of items reported missing. They were in Norman and Bradley's, pawnbrokers, at the time – somewhere they had both gone to raise money on numerous occasions.

The Blue Melodians had not played outside Cambridge, mainly gigging at small local charity events. Socially though, Newman, Potts and others had been further afield and he admitted that he had had to appear before his own tutor, Mr Thatcher, for going to Mildenhall in cars. This reprimand was enough to prompt Newman to leave Cambridge rather than face his family to explain his behaviour.

Potts had already had the idea of going abroad and they had gone as far as getting the forms to apply for passports before abandoning the idea. Potts now partially resurrected it, suggesting that they went away for a month before getting a job. Between them they owned a motorcycle, which they had bought a few days earlier, and thought they would use for transport. At first they also planned to sell their possessions to raise funds but, except for a few items that Potts carried with him, they abandoned this idea after deciding that they would set out for London immediately.

Within twenty-four hours the ill-conceived plan was in disarray; they arrived in the capital at 3.15 p.m. on 24 May and, with nowhere to stay, spent the night on the steps of St Martin-in-the-Fields. During the evening they sold the motorbike for £22 10s but were paid with a cheque that they would not be able to cash until the coming Monday.

They had no accommodation and, even with the cash from the cheque, they found themselves broke again very quickly. Their lifeline came in the form Madge Miller, who they did not know personally but had been told to look up by a mutual friend.

Miller was a 25-year-old dance instructor who lived in Shaftesbury Avenue. By the time they contacted her it was Thursday 29 May and they claimed they had not slept for the previous seven nights. They had run out of money and had spent the previous night walking along the Embankment. They arrived at her flat between two and three in the morning and she took them in. The only money she gave them was enough to get their luggage from Charing Cross Station, but she did feed them and let them sleep in her spare bedroom. They eventually left on Monday 2 June.

In her witness statement she told the jury that on the night of their arrival there had been no milk in the flat so they had drunk tea Russian style and had talked for so long that she had lost track of the time. In the morning Potts had sent her maid out for a loaf of bread and the two young men had left the flat at 11.30. She overheard them talking about meeting a man called Desmond at the Savoy for lunch. Potts hoped this Desmond would give them some money but they came back empty handed. It was never clear whether 'Desmond' even existed.

When they returned to her flat on the Friday night she saw that each of them carried a gun. She asked: 'Are they loaded?' to which one of them replied in the affirmative.

Wondering why they had guns Potts told her, 'We shall need these.' Miller asked them not to load them.

Potts told her that there were problems at college. He often referred to John Newman as Gerald, one of his middle names: he asked, 'Hasn't Gerald told you about the trouble?' Potts went on to say that there was trouble about money, a smashed car and also a man was taking out a warrant for his arrest.

Under questioning from the coroner Newman admitted that he had also owned a revolver. He had bought it in Cambridge and claimed that his sole purpose in owning it was to cover Potts' weapon with the single licence. He also admitted that both of them had threatened to commit suicide with their guns. He assured the coroner that they had not been serious threats. While in London Potts and Newman had run into several acquaintances and the threats of suicide had been a ruse to give the impression that they were desperate and could not face returning to Cambridge. This, they hoped, would discourage anyone from turning them over to their tutors.

Triple shooting tragedy at Cambridge. (Police Illustrated News)

Miller advised them to return to face the music but Potts and Newman went on to spend the weekend with her; she paid for them all to go the cinema twice. They played cards together in the evenings and on Sunday afternoon they walked around Fleet Street and High Holborn. At one point Potts stopped to point out the office where his father worked.

On Saturday Potts sent two letters, one to a girl in Tonbridge, the other to a friend at Cambridge. He told Miller that he planned to see this girl as soon as he had the money to do so.

On Monday, 2 June, after they had risen at about 11 a.m., Miller had a brief conversation with Potts. He said: 'Gerald is going home. I am really glad because I think he is going to have a breakdown. He looks ill.' She checked this with Newman who replied: 'I will be back in two days'. Later that afternoon he telephoned and left the same message with her housekeeper. But Miller did not see either of them again until she read of the shootings and saw Newman at the inquest. Potts and Newman did not leave London, they just felt that they could not impose on their host any further and had another sleepless night on their own.

Meanwhile, on the same Monday, the letter Potts had sent to Cambridge arrived with a third-year undergraduate, Frederick Waterwell Bolton. Bolton had known Potts for a few months after Newman had introduced them. The last time Bolton had seen his friends was 24 May, the day they left college. Newman had come straight from his tutor's rooms and was very agitated. He had asked Bolton to take a letter to Potts, which he said was a demand for £5 from a man at Mildenhall.

Bolton then had a conversation with Potts who said he had wired the man 50s the day before but the letter was a demand for the other 50s. Potts said he only had £1. Bolton kindly agreed to lend him the other £1 10s. Potts also said that he was about to be sent down.

The last time Bolton saw the two was the same afternoon as they were preparing to leave Cambridge on their motorcycle. The letter Bolton received on Monday 2 June read :

Many many thanks for all you did for us when we were leaving. We shall never forget the services of a true friend. Here are things for you to do if you will be so kind. I enclose the pawn ticket for Gerald's watch. You can get it out of 'pop' and wear it yourself, and sell it, pay a bill, and keep the rest for yourself. I enclose a letter, which perhaps you will be kind enough to post. Thanking you for my dress clothes. Pack them up and send the dress suit and the waistcoats to Stephen Morris Esq. *Poste Restant*, Charing Cross Post Office. Can you tactfully send to Mr and Mrs Newman – Gerald is quite safe in London.

Bolton decided to go to Mr Thacker, the censor of Fitzwilliam House,[1] and tell him of the letter. Thacker told Bolton to go to Charing Cross Post Office, to find

Potts and Newman and tell them to return to Cambridge. He said that they had overestimated the seriousness of the trouble they were in and in addition Newman needed to know that his father was seriously ill.

Bolton arrived at the post office at 9 a.m. on Tuesday morning. At 9.40 Potts walked in and was surprised to see him. Bolton told Newton and Potts that they should return to Cambridge, to which Potts said: 'I am going back to Cambridge and I shall be putting my head into a hornet's nest.'

Bolton advised him to cheer up and encouraged him to believe that everything would be all right. He drove them back to Cambridge and, despite Potts's earlier comment, found him to be an extremely cheerful companion. They arrived in Cambridge at just after 1 p.m. and Potts left them outside Fitzwilliam House. In the few minutes that followed he met Wollaston and together they headed for Wollaston's rooms and their final ill-fated meeting.

Bolton was shocked when he heard of the shootings. He said he had always known Potts to be 'brilliant but excitable' but had found him to be very calm on that day.

One of the final witnesses was R.J. Pearson, the Chief Constable, who told the court of the last entry in Sergeant Willis's notebook – it was the serial number of the Webley pistol that was to kill him.

Shortly afterwards the jury retired. It took them only thirty minutes to return with the verdict that Douglas Newton Potts had committed suicide during temporary insanity and that he murdered Wollaston and Willis during temporary insanity.

Chief Constable Pearson and a reporter.
(Cambridgeshire Collection, Cambridge Central Library)

The funerals of all three victims took place on Saturday 7 June. Potts was buried at the borough cemetery in Newmarket Road, Cambridge at 9 a.m. His parents and Revd Church, who conducted the service, were the only mourners present.

In contrast the service held for Alexander Frederick Richmond Wollaston was at 2.30 p.m. in King's College chapel and was attended by a huge number of college staff and members of his family. Wollaston was cremated, and in a rare tribute to their lost tutor the ashes were later placed in the crypt of the chapel. The following brief obituary, which appeared in the next publication of the *Cambridge University Reporter*, does not express the great affection that was clearly felt for Wollaston.

'Died at Cambridge on Tuesday, 3 June 1930, Alexander Frederick Richmond Wollaston, M.A., B. Chir, Fellow and Tutor of King's College, aged 55 years.'

The funeral for Sergeant Francis James Willis took place in his home town of Haverhill. His coffin was taken from his parents' house to the West End Congregational Church, and from there to the burial ground. On its journey it was followed by 120 police officers representing eleven different police forces. His wife was left with a widow's pension of £85 a year. A charitable fund was set up to help Willis's family and public donations exceeded £50.

Potts had been considered to be academically brilliant but it is fair to say that he was not realistic about how to behave or what he could achieve outside his academic life. Newman seemed to find Potts' behaviour to be normal and this may have helped Potts stray further from reality. When they went to London they soon discovered that they were incapable of being independent and their anxiety was compounded by lack of sleep. For Newton, the opportunity to return to Cambridge may have come as a relief; for Potts it clearly did not.

No doubt Mr and Mrs Potts must have spent the rest of their lives wondering what had triggered their son's final bloody outburst and whether it could have been prevented. Perhaps Mr Potts replayed the following exchange in his memory and wondered whether they had truly found the answer.

> Counsel: 'Do you think from your knowledge of your son that in an excitable moment, in a moment of great stress, with the responsibility of being faced with the shame of being taken to the police station and of having to confess to you, that he may have temporarily lost his balance?'
> Potts: 'I think that that is the true story of this – that he was afraid to face me, that he thought he had let me down.'
> Counsel: 'That is your considered opinion?'
> Potts: 'Yes.'
> Counsel: 'Was he always ambitious that you, his father, should be proud of him?'
> Potts: 'Yes, he told me he was going to try and get a fellowship at King's.'

Potts may have had lofty ambitions but Wollaston had realised many of his. He had not married until he was 48, and his chance to raise a family was most cruelly thwarted. In 1977 Wollaston's son, who had been only 4 years old at the time of his father's death, wrote an article for the *Telegraph*'s Sunday magazine. In it he describes the loss his family suffered and the painful way his mother learned of her husband's death while spending a day in London:

The news rocked the college and raced through the town, and before the end of the afternoon it had reached the London papers. My mother, walking in Leicester Square, saw a terrifying headline across the front of the *Evening Standard*: UNDERGRADUATE SHOOTS TUTOR DEAD: AMAZING DRAMA AT CAMBRIDGE. She fumbled for a penny and gave it to the man. 'Read all about it', he said, and she did.

Notes
1 The censor acted as Head of House for non-collegiate students attached to Fitzwilliam House. In 1966 Fitzwilliam House achieved collegiate status.

14

THE DOG WAS THE FIRST TO DIE

On Saturday 28 May 1932 Cambridge was rocked by a multiple murder that is probably better understood now than when it was committed.

Meads End is a large detached house standing on the corner where Hills Avenue meets Hinton Avenue in a quiet suburb of Cambridge. The house was owned by Herbert Tebbutt who lived there with his family; Helen, known by their staff as his wife, Helen's daughter Betty aged 12, and their young boys, Michael, 2 and 1-year-old Dickie.

Herbert Tebbutt had been educated at the Leys School in Cambridge and was a keen cricketer. While in his twenties, before the First World War, he had captained the Cambridgeshire County Cricket Team. Speaking shortly after Tebbutt's death an official from the Cambridgeshire Cricket Association had gone on record to say, 'Mr. Tebbutt was one of the finest bats the county ever had. While at Leys he held the record for the greatest number of runs obtained in a season. Many years ago I played with him for the Y.M.C.A. and other teams.'

Mead's End.
(Cambridgeshire
Collection, Cambridge
Central Library)

Mr Tebbutt as a young man. (Cambridgeshire Collection, Cambridge Central Library)

Tebbutt was only 46 years old but had already retired from Bailey and Tebbutt, the brewing business he had inherited from his father. He had been actively involved in the business before selling it to Messrs Greene, King and Sons in 1928. He had also inherited £20,000. His total inheritance made him a comparatively wealthy man.

He occupied himself with the leisurely pursuits of shooting, playing golf and motoring. He was also a frequent visitor to the Cherry Hinton Constitutional Club where until February he had been on the committee.

Helen was 38. She had been born in Hearn City, California and her maiden name was Jenks. After arriving in England she had married a man named Walter Williams with whom she had had two children, Bryan and Elizabeth, known as Betty. By the mid-1920s she was estranged from Williams and had taken the children to live with her aunt and uncle in Chirk near Wrexham.

She later moved to Liverpool where her mother was then living in 1928, when Bryan and Betty were aged 13 and 8, she left Liverpool and moved to Cambridge to take up the post of hotel manageress. Her daughter stayed with her while her son remained with family. It is not known why Helen chose Cambridge; there is no evidence that she knew Herbert Tebbutt beforehand and was thought to have met him shortly after she took up her new position.

The relationship between Tebbutt and Helen Williams developed quickly, but not without complications. Tebbutt was also a married man but soon after meeting

Williams, he bought her a house called Little St Bernard's in Trumpington. He was open about the affair. His wife briefly attempted to save their marriage, but after discovering that Williams was pregnant she filed for divorce.

The divorce case was reported in the *Cambridge Daily News* of 5 December 1929 and stated: 'in the Divorce Division yesterday, before Mr Justice Bateson and a common jury, Mrs Alice Tebbutt of Meads End, Hills Avenue, Cambridge petitioned for a decree nisi for the dissolution of her marriage with Mr Herbert Charles Tebbutt, on the grounds of his adultery with Mrs Helen Margaret Williams of Little St Bernards, Shelford Road, Cambridge, who intervened in this suit.

Both the respondent and the intervener filed answers denying the charge, but had now intimated that they would not contest the case further, and the suit came on as an undefended petition.

The parties were married in July 1913, the petitioner then being a widow of Ealing. They lived at various addresses and finally at Meads End. From 1921 to 1928 the marriage was unhappy and the respondent left his wife in April of that year.

Evidence was given by the petitioner and a private detective.

The jury found that the respondent and the intervener had committed adultery and his Lordship granted a decree nisi with costs.'

The decree absolute was granted on 3 June 1931. After the divorce Tebbutt found it difficult to regain possession of Meads End and its furniture from his former wife. This was eventually resolved and Tebbutt was ordered to pay her maintenance of £500 per year from his estimated annual income of £900. He appealed against this decision and the amount was reduced to £300 per year. Even with this reduction, his lifestyle and his family's living expenses were still eating into his capital. Between the time of the divorce and Tebbutt's death his

Mrs Williams (left), Betty Williams and Michael Tebbutt (centre) and Anthony Tebbutt (right).
(All three photographs Cambridgeshire Collection, Cambridge Central Library)

Mr Tebbutt not long before the shooting. (Cambridgeshire Collection, Cambridge Central Library)

solicitor, Mr Albert George Rickards Alexander, described the amount of alimony he paid out to his ex-wife as 'a considerable amount'. Despite this Tebbutt was still in arrears by £250.

The finances surrounding his divorce seemed to anger Tebbutt rather than worry him, and he particularly objected to the section in the order that made provision for his ex-wife for her lifetime and meant that she would be paid from his estate in the event that he pre-deceased her.

Mostly, however, he focused his attention on his new family and was very fond of all three children and was often seen taking them out in his car. The family employed a gardener and two maids, Phyllis Henderson and Florence Southgate. Henderson lived in Oak Street, Cambridge but Southgate, who was a local girl, lived at the house with the rest of the family. She had been with the family for four years, while Henderson had been employed for the previous six weeks to help with the children.

Although Henderson was happy in her position she was due to leave as she needed to go into hospital. She hoped to return later, but in her absence the Tebbutts had hired a young girl from Downham Market named Olga Dudley.

In the weeks leading up to Saturday 28 May a few small and seemingly insignificant events took place. And certainly from the perspective of Henderson and Southgate nothing occurred that warned them about the fast approaching tragedy.

They perhaps thought it was strange that Dudley did not arrive on Wednesday 25 May, but then they had heard that her mother had telephoned and Tebbutt had jotted down the following message for his partner; 'Olga ill, cannot come till tomorrow.' Maybe they assumed Dudley was still unwell when there was still no sign of her by Saturday.

The two maids were unlikely to be privy to conversations that Tebbutt was having with his solicitor. Tebbutt had been ordered to leave securities to cover half of the annual payments due to his former wife and he had failed to do so. On that same Wednesday Alexander warned Tebbutt that a writ of judgment was about to be issued against him. Tebbutt promised to drop the securities off at the solicitor's office on Friday, but never did.

Both the maids were aware though of the event which Southgate thought had distressed Tebbutt. He was keen on shooting and kept three dogs including a spaniel and a cross-bred retriever. He was particularly fond of the retriever, which he had owned for fourteen years, and that morning had asked Mr Bennett, a local vet, to put the dog to sleep. Bennett had come to Meads End and taken the animal away. Southgate was not absolutely sure that this had greatly upset her master, but noted that if anyone mentioned the dog being destroyed 'tears came into his eyes and he could not speak for a few minutes'.

After the vet's visit Tebbutt drove into town and settled bills at the Rock Hotel and D.H. Halls, the boot-maker, where he collected two pairs of shoes that had been repaired. He also dropped in to the Cherry Hinton Constitutional Club where he was described as 'cheery as ever' and had one drink, but refused a second that another member offered to buy.

The family were due to go to on holiday; Tebbutt had hired a bungalow on the golf estate at Gorleston-on-Sea and they planned to stay there for a few weeks. During the evening of Friday 27 May Tebbutt had telephoned to confirm that they would arrive at about 5 p.m. on Saturday 28 May. On the following morning he returned home at about 12.15, in time to drive the two maids to the station. It had been arranged that they would catch the 1.20 p.m. train while the family would travel to Gorleston by car.

Back at the house he found the children dressed, but Williams not yet ready to leave. He told the maids to wait in the car, which was still in the garage about 100 yards from the house. As Southgate left she remembered that the daughter, Betty, was upstairs and the two babies were in their prams in the kitchen while Williams was busy putting a telephone call through to the general post office.

She sat with Henderson for several minutes, and then they heard three shots, followed by a scream and more shots. At first they thought the shots came from the orchard but realising that the sound was too close Southgate said: 'It's coming from the kitchen. Surely he hasn't shot the children.'

The distraught maid ran into the house via the back door and was faced with a scene worse than anything she could have imagined. Dick was in his pram; his legs were moving but blood was pouring from his face. Betty lay on the floor.

She ran back out and told her companion, 'They have been shot. They are on the floor.' Both girls re-entered the house and Henderson saw that 'Betty was lying on the floor, her head in a pool of blood. Dick was in a perambulator. Michael was in another perambulator, their heads down. They were bleeding from the nose and mouth.'

As they did not know where the Tebbutts were and whether there was an ongoing danger they ran back from the house to summon help. They returned with a neighbour and the milkman, Joseph Allington from Stetchworth Dairies. Several neighbours had heard shots but had ignored them as Tebbutt often fired at birds in the garden.

They found Tebbutt and Williams in the hall. Both were dead with bullet wounds to the head. The telephone receiver was hanging from its cable as if the shootings had occurred while the phone was in use. In fact the switchboard operator who had been connecting Williams' call had heard the shots but had been unable to do anything to help.

Although the telephone was damaged Allington used it to call the police and, on seeing that the two younger children were alive, he rang a local doctor, Albert McMasters from Hills Road. At the inquest the Chief Constable, R.J. Pearson, publicly thanked him for his actions.

McMasters arrived shortly after 1.00 p.m. and found both boys still breathing. Sadly though he was unable to help them. One died five minutes later and the other survived for only another forty.

The story made the afternoon edition of the *Cambridge Daily News* under the headline 'Five Dead in Cambridge Tragedy' and also made the national papers with *The Times* carrying a small piece headed 'Five Persons Found Shot'.

The inquest was held on Monday 30 May at the old Police Court in Cambridge's Guild Hall and opened by the borough coroner, G.A. Wootten. W.B. Frampton, from Squires and Co. solicitors, represented the executors and relatives and Grafton Pryor represented Alice Tebbutt, Herbert Tebbutt's first wife (he was the solicitor who had unsuccessfully defended Frederick Seekings at his 1913 murder trial).

The first witness called was James Scott who had taken photos in the hallway and kitchen of Meads End. Inspector Sharman also described the scene. Shortly before 1.00 p.m. on Saturday the police station had received an urgent call from Allington and Sharman had taken four officers to Meads End. He said in his statement that 'they found a man lying face downwards, with his head in a pool of blood. The man had a bullet wound in the right temple and his face was bluish black. Quite close to the man lay the body of Mrs Williams, who had a wound on her left cheek, and her face was covered with blood.'

In the kitchen he had found the three children:

> The girl was lying on her back, five feet from the door with a wound in one eye. Two feet from her head was a pushchair, and in that chair was the elder of the two babies who had serious wounds to the side of the head. Quite close to the pushchair was a pram containing a child of about eighteen months. That child had serious wounds to the left side of the head.

Williams' brother, George Albert Jenks, identified his sister's body. He worked as a grocer's assistant at the Army and Navy Stores in Victoria Street, London and confirmed that his sister had still been married at the time of her death. Her husband was a Walter Williams, but the witness confirmed that Helen had already separated from him by the time he had last seen his sister. Jenks had last seen Betty when she was about 5 years old, but was able to identify her body positively.

Some of the most distressing testimony came from the two maids. Henderson was the first of the two to take the stand and, after confirming her personal and

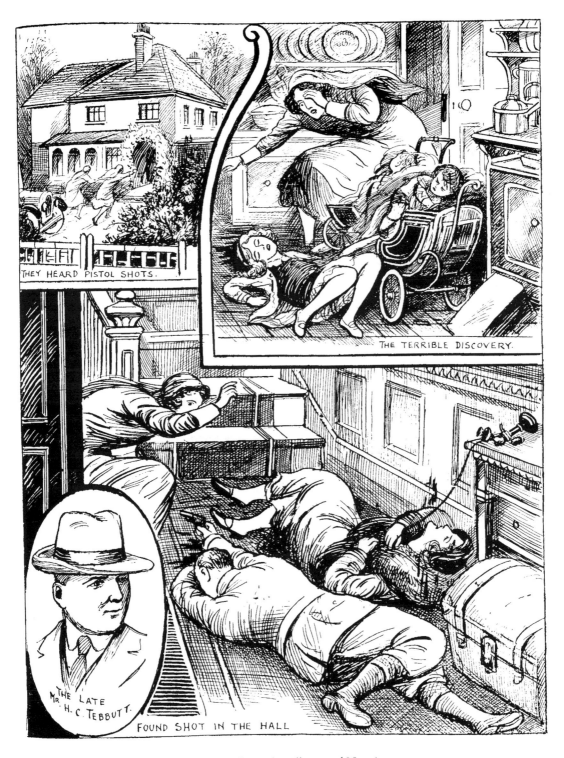

THEY HEARD PISTOL SHOTS.

THE TERRIBLE DISCOVERY.

THE LATE
Mr. H. C. TEBBUTT.

FOUND SHOT IN THE HALL

Terrible shooting tragedy in a Cambridge villa. (Police Illustrated News)

employment details, she identified the bodies of the two youngest children as Michael Charles Hazeldene Tebbutt Williams, aged 2 years and 10 months and Anthony Richard Hazeldene Tebbutt aged 1½. He was known by the family as Dickie and they were, as far as she was aware, both sons of Williams.

She testified that on Saturday 28 May she had risen at her usual time of 7.30 a.m. and had breakfasted with the three children and the other maid. Mrs Tebbutt (as she knew her) came down at 9 a.m. Just prior to that she had seen Mr Tebbutt, who was still in his pyjamas, come down to pick up his post before returning upstairs.

Henderson explained that the family were preparing to go on holiday and that she was expecting to be replaced. The coroner asked why she was leaving them to which she informed him that she was going into hospital.

'You were not at all unhappy?'

'Oh no.'

'As far as you know, who was to take your place?'

'Miss Olga Dudley.'

'Should she have arrived earlier than this?'

'Yes. She was to have come on the previous Wednesday, but she did not do so.'

'Do you know if Mr Tebbutt sent a telegram to her?'

'He said he had.'

'He received a reply stating that she was ill and would come the following day?'

'Yes.'

Henderson confirmed that she thought there had been a misunderstanding over the engagement of Dudley. She added that Williams had been annoyed about it, 'but nothing more than usual. Between 9.30 and 9.45 Olga's mother rang up and Mr Tebbutt answered her. Later, at about 10.30 a.m. Mrs Dudley rang up and Mrs Williams answered that call. Mrs Williams asked if Olga was better. She had to ask the question several times because Mrs Dudley did not seem to understand. She seemed surprised.'

The coroner asked: 'Did Mrs Williams tell you that Mrs Dudley said she had received a telegram telling Olga not to come?'

Phyllis replied: 'Yes' and also explained that Williams had told Mrs Dudley that she still expected her daughter to start work but would not accept her unless she brought proof of the telegram.

It seems that Williams was not content to leave the matter there and was suspicious. She decided to ring the general post office for confirmation of the telegram's existence and origin. It was no secret that she was placing a call to the G.P.O. and was on the hall telephone as Tebbutt instructed the maids to wait in the car.

Henderson had not been in Tebbutt's employ for long and could not give the inquest much of an insight into the relationship between him and his lover. She had overheard one argument but thought that there was nothing about their relationship that pointed to anything but normal married life.

Southgate, however, had been at Meads End for four years and knew more about the family's daily habits than her colleague. She explained that it would be typical of Tebbutt to stay up until 2 a.m. and often the couple would not take breakfast until between ten and ten-thirty each morning. Tebbutt would spend time in the garden in the mornings, or often go out, but arrive back in time for lunch at 1.30 p.m. After lunch he would often have a sleep before going out again. He would arrive home 'at all hours', but Southgate was sure that this caused no trouble and he would have another nap downstairs before retiring to bed at his usual time.

As far as she knew, Tebbutt's activities outside the house consisted solely of shooting, golf and occasional visits to his club. She thought she had never seen him drunk but admitted that the week's empty bottles would include two or three of his whisky bottles. She said that Tebbutt and Williams had quarrelled occasionally, most often at night-time. She described Tebbutt's temper as 'hasty', but said their arguments were mostly little tiffs.

According to the coroner's opening statement the inquest was going to hear 'that the deceased man and woman frequently quarrelled' but this was not borne out in the witness statements and there was no evidence to suggest that the couple were unhappy with the relationship.

There was nothing to indicate that anything in Southgate's statement was played down through loyalty. She was clearly very fond of the family with whom she had lived at Little St Bernards before moving to Meads End. She said: 'I used to love being there.'

On the subject of Dudley, her statement confirmed Henderson's. She seemed sure that Williams felt that it was Dudley that might be the one being deceptive and not Tebbutt. She knew that her employer had asked the new recruit to prove that she had received the telegrams. Southgate had also overheard her employers discussing the matter and there was no sign of any annoyance.

She broke down when she described hearing the shots and the scream then finding the children in the kitchen. She was crying too much to answer questions for a short time.

The coroner asked her why she had said to her colleague: 'Surely he hasn't shot the children' and she explained that it was only her response to the scream and the fact that the shots came from inside the house. There was no other reason. In fact in her entire statement there were only two incidents that pointed to possible undercurrents in the Tebbutt household.

Southgate knew little of Tebbutt's divorce from his wife but was present one day when Williams came out of the kitchen. She and Tebbutt had been arguing and she said that it was over nothing, but he was worried about the money he had to pay his ex-wife. According to Southgate, Williams then said that he 'would rather shoot himself than she should have the money'.

The coroner raised the second point when he asked her what she knew of Tebbutt's revolver. She stated that two or three times when she had made the bed she had found it under his pillow, and one night, when he was looking at it, Williams had said: 'Don't mess about with that'.

Inspector Sharman was called. After describing the state of the victims and their locations, which he and his officers had found on their arrival at Meads End, he explained how they had gone on to search the house. In the hall the telephone was on its hook, but the mouthpiece and the aluminium disc were missing. It was logical that the handset had been replaced in its cradle as it had been used by Allington to call for help. There was a bullet mark on the mouthpiece and the paper disc where the telephone number was written was also torn.

Inspector Sharman told the inquest, 'I searched the body of the man and noticed a whisky flask full in the right hip pocket of his trousers. In the right trouser pocket I found a seven-chambered revolver of .22 calibre, fully loaded.'

'On searching the body you had to be particularly careful in getting the revolver out?' asked the coroner.

'Yes', Sharman replied. 'It was necessary to cut the trousers before we could take the revolver out. Further examination of the body made it necessary to be very careful. The right arm was doubled up and the hand was not visible. From the position we suspected there was a weapon in the hand, and when the body was moved a German automatic pistol was found clasped in the right hand. The fingers were round the butt, and the thumb was on the trigger.'

According to Sharman seven cartridges were found. *The Times* reported on the following day: 'On the ground floor were found 50 bullet cases', which was simply not the case.

Most of the bodies had entry and exit wounds although Tebbutt himself only had the entry wound. The aluminium disc missing from the telephone's receiver was found under Tebbutt's body and under Williams was a broken hair slide and the missing mouthpiece from the telephone.

Before the inquest Sharman had made searches of both the firearms and trophy registers of the borough and county and could find no record that Tebbutt's firearms were licensed. A box of .22 cartridges was found in Tebbutt's pocket and further ammunition was discovered upstairs. The only other item of note found on Tebbutt's body was a cheque for £10, drawn to the bearer on Lloyds Bank.

In Sharman's opinion Williams had been shot first, and although it would have been possible for Betty to have been shot from the hallway, Tebbutt would have entered the kitchen to kill the boys. He found an empty bullet case in the pushchair and confirmed that it had come from Tebbutt's revolver, which had been fired at close range. Apart from a bullet hole in the hood of the perambulator and the damaged telephone, which accounted for two cases, the other five bullets had all been fired into the victim's heads. The final bullet had been fired into his right temple.

To ascertain the extent that the divorce may have had on Tebbutt's state of mind, his solicitor Albert Alexander was called. He explained that the first Mrs Tebbutt had brought the proceedings and, although Mr Tebbutt had entered a defence, he had not contested them. Tebbutt had not been happy at the amount and terms of the settlement.

It seems that Tebbutt had no real grounds for withholding either the £300 annual maintenance or the associated securities, although Alexander admitted that the amount had been calculated 'rather by default' and that 'certain papers were not filed and the information before the [divorce] court was not complete'.

On the subject of the size of the settlement the coroner also asked whether it would have left Tebbutt with sufficient funds to maintain Meads End. Alexander explained that it had left Tebbutt needing to delve into his capital to make it possible. He had been trying to get in touch with his client to persuade him to hand over the securities. The last time he had seen him he had warned him that a writ of attachment was about to be issued and that this could result in Tebbutt's arrest.

A four-day notice had already been served on Tebbutt and there was no excuse for him not to have obeyed the order. Evidence heard later in the day showed that the writ would most probably have been executed on Monday 30 May.

Alexander's opinion of Tebbutt's temper corresponded with the statements made by other witnesses; he had been quick to anger, but equally quick to cool off. Alexander had also helped to draw up Tebbutt's will, which made careful provision for Williams and Tebbutt's two young sons.

The will had been discovered among Tebbutt's personal effects and included a codicil that which had been added on 15 May 1932. Perhaps because Tebbutt seemed to be avoiding his solicitor, it was not Alexander who had been the witness to the change.

Mr and Mrs Martin, the steward and stewardess at the Constitutional Club, had witnessed the addition. Martin stated that Tebbutt had seemed quite normal and had remarked that it was only fair to 'fix things up' for those that came after

Bailey & Tebbutt Brewery just after its sale to Greene King. (Cambridgeshire Collection, Cambridge Central Library)

him. The codicil made provision for Betty Williams in addition to the provision
he had already made for his own two children.

The *Cambridge Daily News* printed a couple of paragraphs relating to
Tebbutt's temper, the first was purportedly the observations of 'a member' of the
Constitutional Club who observed that Tebbutt was a man 'who got every
pleasure out of life but of late had developed a rather uncertain temper'. Tebbutt
apparently 'always carried a revolver and would often flourish it, even when he
was in business at Messrs Bailey and Tebbutt's brewery'.

This was followed by the following paragraph: 'An example of Mr Tebbutt's
temper was shown recently when a person called in connection with the divorce
proceedings and not only had a dog set on him but water thrown from the first
floor window.'

Alexander's opinion of Tebbutt seemed at odds with this; he thought the
household at Meads End was normal and that his client seemed like a caring
family man with nothing but good things to say about Williams and the children.
From Alexander's knowledge of Tebbutt the described action seemed totally out
of character.

When Wootten summed up he said that it was clear that Tebbutt had shot the
others before turning the gun on himself and that a man who carried unlicensed
firearms was likely to be a danger, both to himself and to others. Wootten also
accepted that the divorce and outstanding problems with the settlement could
have preyed on Tebbutt's mind, although he felt that there was nothing in his
current living arrangements that seemed likely to have driven him to such drastic
action. Addressing the jury he said: 'I am going to ask you to say that the said
Herbert Charles Tebbutt did feloniously and wilfully and with malice
aforethought, kill and murder the said Helen Margaret Williams, Elizabeth
Rosemary Williams, Michael Charles Hazeldene Tebbutt Williams and Anthony
Richard Hazeldene Tebbutt. It is also for you to say that he subsequently
committed suicide by shooting himself. I think perhaps you might mercifully say
in this case he did it while temporarily insane.' The jury did not retire and were
happy to agree with the coroner's assessment of the case.

The funeral of all five took place on Monday 30 May at the borough cemetery
in Newmarket Road, Cambridge. Tebbutt was buried first without a chapel
service and only a short service at the grave. Alexander and a few friends
attended, leaving two wreaths and a lily cross at the grave.

For Williams and the children there was a chapel service where just close
friends and family were admitted. The mourners included Helen's brother, George
Jenks, and his wife. Two girls from Betty's school attended and brought a simple
wreath. The four coffins were taken to a different part of the cemetery from
Tebbutt's. Florence Southgate followed the children's coffins and cried
throughout. Michael and Dickie were buried in one grave, while Williams and
Betty were buried together in a third grave.

There is nothing to suggest that the verdict from the inquest was in any way
incorrect, but since this type of crime has gained more attention so has the

understanding of what motivates fathers to commit these rare but terrible crimes. The fact that Herbert Tebbutt went about his business in a seemingly normal and responsible way was used by the inquest as an indication that he had not planned to kill the family but did so during a 'brainstorm'.

It could be argued that the opposite is true: it is not uncommon for suicides to put their affairs in order and the amendments to Tebbutt's will could have been put to use if one of the children had in fact survived.

Tebbutt's seemingly normal behaviour was also no indicator; many fathers who have killed in this way have done so after successfully repressing their fears and stresses until they feel their problems have grown too large to cope with and equally too complex for it to be worth confiding in anyone else.

As close as Tebbutt appeared to be to Williams he may have felt that his dwindling assets and the lifestyle adjustment that his poor change in fortune was beginning to indicate were a threat to their relationship. She had been upset at leaving Little St Bernards and it had been he who insisted on moving the family to Meads End; it is therefore reasonable to assume that the possibility of losing Meads End and moving the family for a second time was extremely hard for him to contemplate.

Home Office statistics for 2001 showed a 40 per cent rise in the number of children and teenagers killed since the previous twelve month period, most of these deaths occurred in domestic situations. These figures were inflated by a significant rise in the numbers of fathers killing their children, (filicide[1] or familicide),[2] and, in the United States, figures show that on average the country has fifty cases of familicide per year.

Recent research has uncovered the following trends that apply to fathers who commit familicide. They are:

Caucasians in their 30s or 40s.
Bad at handling stress.
Possessive of their families.
Often depressed or drunk.
Controlling.
Often kill with a knife or gun that they have owned for some time.
Believe that their families are completely dependent on them.

Although some people perceive these crimes as largely a modern phenomenon it is clear from the case of Herbert Tebbutt that he fitted the profile. Fathers who commit these acts are often under the illusion that they are doing the best for all concerned. We will never know what was going on in Tebbutt's mind, but for the reader this must be a case that echoes with the most needless waste of life.

Notes
1 Filicide is the murder of a child by parents.
2 Familicide is the murder of an entire family.

15

TO LOVE, HONOUR BUT MOSTLY OBEY

On 9 March 1935 Sybil Emily Worthington died. But there was never any question that anyone except her husband, Walter Osmond Worthington, had killed her. After an inquest, trial and unsuccessful appeal Walter Worthington became the last Cambridgeshire man to be executed: on 10 July 1935 he was hanged at Bedford gaol. The grounds for his appeal, and the mystery which endures to this day, was whether he had meant to kill her or, as his defence had argued, had he just intended to kill himself.

Sybil Worthington (née Parker) was born in June 1907 and was from a large family from Streatham, London. She worked in Bruton Street, London for Norman Hartnell, the rising star in the world of couture. His most famous creation was the gown worn by Queen Elizabeth at her coronation in 1953.

One of her sisters, Bertha, was married to John Churchill Wright and they lived in Broughton, Huntingdonshire. They ran the village shop and later also took over the Crown pub next door. It was during a visit to her sister that Sybil met a local widower, Walter Worthington. He was thirty years older than her and had lived in Broughton for about five years. Worthington was originally from a village between Southend-on-Sea and Wickford in Essex but his first wife and one of their thirteen children were buried in Broughton.

After a brief courtship Sybil and Walter were married by the vicar of St Anne's, South Lambeth, in November 1933 and moved to Broughton to live at Worthington's home, The Meads. Three of Walter's children also lived there with them – teenagers David and Ronald and 4-year-old Bobby.

Sybil, new to the area, initially spent much time at her sister's pub, the Crown, which was just a few hundred yards from her home. Also living at the pub were Mr and Mrs Wright's son, Lionel, 22, who worked as a local omnibus driver and Mr Worthington's youngest child, aged 5. Lionel had lived in Canada for a while and returned to England in September 1933, in time to attend the wedding of Sybil and Walter. The first visit he made to The Meads was soon after the wedding but, as he was not made to feel welcome at the house, he did not visit again until a comment from his father prompted him to go.

The Worthingtons rarely went out and even their children were very secretive about their home life. As 1934 progressed the Wrights had seen less and less of

The Meads at Broughton. (Author's Collection)

Sybil, and Bertha, who had always been close to her sister, became concerned. On 17 December that year Mr Wright visited the Worthingtons to find out whether there was a problem.

Sybil appeared to look very ill; she was pale and haggard with heavy black shadows under her eyes. Mr Wright asked her if she had been unwell. Worthington replied on her behalf saying that she was quite healthy. Sybil though stayed silent and so Mr Wright asked why she had not been to see her sister for almost six months. But again it was Walter Worthington who spoke: 'I will not allow her to come,' he said.

When Mr Wright asked why this was the case Worthington continued: 'I won't let her come because Lionel is there.' Worthington claimed that Lionel had insulted Sybil in the week after their marriage; but he would not say what it was. Wright decided that he would send up his wife and son to sort it out.

Bertha and Lionel visited the next day but when they arrived at The Meads Worthington denied having said anything to Wright. Worthington walked across the room and picked up his shotgun and held it in a 'threatening manner'. When Lionel told him to put it down he did. At that point John Wright arrived to tell Lionel that someone was waiting for him and the family departed.

Another of Sybil's siblings was soon to intervene in this increasingly unhappy marriage. Ivor Parker's family had made a visit to Broughton over Christmas and Sybil went to the Crown to see them off. Ivor walked her home and, when they arrived back at The Meads, he complained to Worthington that Sybil was not being treated well enough. His understanding was that Worthington had accused his wife of being seen home by a farm labourer on a previous night. In actual fact it had been Ivor and his wife who had walked her back home.

Worthington replied: 'I know old man. I am so fond of her. That makes me very jealous.' He went on to admit that he had treated her badly and did not know why he had forbidden her to go the Crown to see her sister.

Ivor suggested that John Wright could go to The Meads to pick her up and, after she had visited, drop her off again. Worthington agreed to this. Ivor refused to shake hands with Worthington however, and said he would only do so when he was convinced that his sister was once again living happily.

Sybil did restart her visits to the Crown but it was evident that her home life had not greatly improved. In January 1935 she stayed with the Wrights for a week. Whether Sybil and Lionel were genuinely close or whether Walter let his jealousy towards the younger man spin needlessly out of control is not known. Lionel always denied an affair between himself and Sybil, but what is clear is that Walter became obsessed with the idea that his young wife was being unfaithful with other men. The primary focus of his concern was directed at his wife's nephew.

Lionel bought a motorcycle on 8 January 1935, and the idea that Sybil may have gone out on it became a preoccupation of Walter's. Lionel later swore that he had never taken Sybil out on it.

At 7 p.m. on Saturday 9 March the three boys were at home with their father and stepmother. The two eldest, David and Ronald, were sitting in the lounge when a fight broke out between their parents who were in the kitchen at the time. The argument was because Sybil was planning to go out for the evening and Walter objected.

When Worthington came into the lounge he was carrying a double-barrelled shotgun, which he broke open. He looked into the breach, most likely to check whether it was loaded, then shut it again. Worthington walked to the end of the room and put the gun in the corner. But he was restless and almost as soon as he had done this he returned to the gun, moved it closer to the fire and sat in a nearby chair.

The boys heard Sybil call out from the kitchen: 'Is my coat in there?'

Her husband replied: 'It's in here on the settee.'

A few moments after this Sybil came into the living room to get her garment. She began putting it on as she left the room, but her husband called out after her: 'Stand back. What's on tonight? You are going for a motorbike ride, aren't you?' Sybil did not answer him.

Within moments a shot had been fired. Worthington had fired as he stood with his back to the door, blocking his wife's exit from the house. She dropped to the floor and Walter paused for just long enough to prop the gun in the recess behind the door. Neither boy saw their father actually shoot the gun but Ronald immediately realised what had happened and asked his father why he had done it.

Worthington did not answer but told the boys that he was going to see Revd Alfred Stearn, the rector of Broughton. He walked into the hall and put on his coat and hat, said goodbye to Ronald and passed the boy a key which he said must be handed over to the police.

Worthington left the Meads and just after 7.30 p.m. flagged down a passing lorry and asked the driver to take him straight to the nearest police station saying that there was 'some trouble at home'. The driver, Reginald Arthur Thompson, thought his passenger seemed agitated but in spite of this, and his passenger's pleas not to stop, Thompson pulled over at the shop next door to the Crown to buy groceries and cigarettes.

Worthington scrambled out of the cab and hurried away. At just before eight he arrived at the rectory and was shown into the study. His opening comment was: 'Rector, I have shot my wife. Take me to the police station.'

Revd Stearn drove Worthington to St Ives. Along the way Worthington rambled on about Sybil, saying how much he loved her and that he had discovered that she had been unfaithful to him and that he did not understand how she could have betrayed him when he loved her so.

When they arrived at the police station they were met by Constable Worby. Stearn told the officer that Worthington had shot his wife. When Worby asked Worthington whether she was dead, Worthington kept repeating that he was afraid she was. The constable called for a senior officer, Inspector Hodson. By the time Hodson arrived Worthington was in a clearly distressed state. Hodson grabbed hold of Worthington's arm and asked what was the matter.

Worthington replied: 'I have shot my wife.'

Hodson warned him that he was making a serious statement and would be wise to say nothing further but Worthington continued: 'I must. She wanted to go out and I didn't want her to. I put the gun up and there I am afraid and deeply sorry for it – I have left a letter for you in the bureau. My son has got the key.'

Worthington was searched and was found to have two live cartridges in his pockets. He was detained at St Ives while Hodson and another constable went to The Meads to confirm the story.

They were not the first on the scene, however. For some reason Mrs Wright had been concerned about her sister. Two of the pub's customers, Ernest Harding and Mr Rignall, went to The Meads with Stearn's son soon joining them. Ernest found 6-year-old Bobby with Sybil's body. He took the little boy from the room and handed him over to Stearn's son to look after.

The police found Sybil Worthington's body where she had fallen. She was wearing her coat, which was not done up, and lying in a pool of blood. She had been shot through the left breast. There was a hole in the left breast of her coat, which showed scorch marks. This made it obvious that the shot had been fired from close range. There was also a similar but clean-cut hole in her jacket.

The post mortem, carried out by Dr Grove on 15 March, confirmed that the heart and left lung were lacerated and that the shot had entered about 1½in left of the nipple and had penetrated as far as the back of the spine. In his opinion Sybil had died instantly. The victim had been 5ft 2in tall and the gun had been fired at a slight downwards angle from within a foot of her.

The gun was found in the recess where it had been stashed. The right barrel contained a discharged cartridge, while the left barrel was fully cocked and contained a live cartridge. Hodson unlocked the bureau and found a bottle of fluid and several papers, including a letter written by Worthington.

An extract from the letter read: 'I beg your pardon for all this trouble but please sift this thing out. Please arrange for the fluid in the bottle to be analysed. He is the cause of this tragedy.'

It was clear from the full letter that the 'he' in question was Lionel Wright. The letter concluded: 'Once more I apologise. W. Worthington. P.S. I cannot endure this any longer, as I have been abused by Lionel Wright. I have not been hasty. My wife left me on 24 January for the reason of spending the night at The Crown Inn. She has almost collapsed when I have accused her, and hung her head, and had nothing to say.'

Another letter addressed to Worthington was from a London firm. It referred to a diaphragm or Dutch Cap, which was mentioned in the subsequent news-paper coverage as just 'an instrument'. It was a popular form of contraception in the 1930s. In his letter Worthington explained that the pessary had been missing and he was sure that she had been using it with someone else. Hodson took the bottle to the public analyst at Cambridge but his findings are not known.

The inquest was held at the rectory at Broughton on the afternoon of Monday 11 March. A week later the funeral took place at Streatham cemetery. The same vicar who had married them conducted the ceremony and many of Mrs Worthington's friends and relatives attended, including former colleagues from Norman Hartnell's.

In an all-day hearing before magistrates at the St Ives Police Court on Tuesday 26 March, Worthington pleaded not guilty: 'I did not intend to hurt her. It was an accident.' He was then committed for trial at the next Huntingdonshire Assizes.

Worthington's trial at Huntingdon Assizes began in mid-May. The prosecution pointed out that the first time Worthington had claimed the shooting to be an accident was on 26 March, seventeen days after his wife's death. But counsel was careful to tell the jury that, even had it been an accident and he had brandished the gun to threaten his wife when it went off, it would still amount to manslaughter because he would have been committing an unlawful act when he pointed it at her.

A gunsmith, William Adkin from Bedford, was called as an expert witness. He said that the gun was of Belgian manufacture and explained that it was slightly faulty and would require more pressure on the trigger than usual to make it fire. The average pull required to discharge a gun of this type was between 4 and 4½lb but Worthington's required 6lb. This made it highly unlikely that the gun could go off accidentally; the trigger would need to be physically pulled quite hard.

Two key witnesses were Worthington's own sons; David aged 16 and Ronald aged 13. They explained what had happened on the evening of their stepmother's death. Ronald in particular struggled to give evidence.

The rector, Revd Stearn, was also called to give evidence. This was not just based on the events of 9 March but because he appeared to know Worthington better than anyone else. Stearn described Worthington as a man who was 'very, very' devoted to his wife and extremely fond of his children. When Worthington's first wife had died Stearn had known him well enough to accompany him into town to do some shopping. He found Worthington to be a very sensitive man. At one point the accused had told him that he had left the door open all night hoping that Sybil would return. This was thought to have been in January, when she went to stay at the Crown for a week.

As Stearn gave this evidence Worthington appeared to become very distressed.

When it was his turn to take the stand Worthington was very precise about his wife's movements during her last week. The detail to which he had noted the time of her trips from the house appeared to border on the obsessive. He recalled that on Monday 4 March she had gone to the Crown at 3 p.m. and returned at 6.20 p.m. On the Tuesday she had gone to a concert at 7 p.m. and he had picked her up at

Walter Worthington. (Author's Collection)

10.45 p.m. while on the Thursday she had again gone to the Crown at 3 p.m. but this time had not returned until five past ten. When Saturday arrived and she told him that she was planning to go out again he objected, saying that she had already been out during the week. But she had made up her mind to go and walked away.

He then claimed that it was in these next minutes that he wrote his note to the police and said that his intention was to kill himself if his wife would not listen to reason. It was only moments later, when Sybil and Walter were next face to face, that the fatal shot was fired.

'I was staggered. I did not think it would go off,' he told the court.

Under cross-examination Worthington went into more detail about his planned suicide. Mr Oliver for the prosecution asked he were jealous of his wife. 'I did not like my wife going to the Crown,' Worthington replied. Oliver proceeded to ask Worthington a string of questions.

'Were you jealous of Lionel Wright?'

'Yes, I had reason to be.'

'Do you remember telling Mr Parker that shortly after your marriage Lionel had insulted your wife?'

'I never said such a thing.'

'Is his evidence untrue?'

'Yes.'

'Did you hear evidence of the conversation with you?'

'Yes.'

'Is that true?'

'No.'

'Did Lionel Wright say to you "I believe my father sooner than you"?'

'He never mentioned it.'

'Did you pick up the gun then?'

'Yes.'

'Why?'

'Because he threatened me. He used verbal threats.'

'What did he say?'

'He said he would take it out of me.'

'And you picked up the gun for self protection?'

'The gun was not loaded. I would have struck him with it if he had hit me.'

'On 9 March you had not been shooting that day?'

'No.'

'Had you had these cartridges a long time?'

'Since September.'

'Do you shoot birds?'

'I never shot the gun. It was a birthday present. The cartridges were sent with the gun.'

'And this evening your wife wanted to go out and you did not want her to?'

'No.'

'Are you asking the jury to believe you loaded the gun to shoot yourself?'

'I do.'

'Did you consider how you were going to shoot yourself?'

'No.'

'It is a difficult thing to shoot yourself with is it not?'

'I don't know.'

'Have you ever made that suggestion in any public place before today?'

'No.'

'You have never made that suggestion before?'

'I was not asked to make a statement.'

'Do you say the letters were written while your wife was upstairs?'

'Yes.'

'You did make up your mind there was going to be a tragedy?'

'I intended to shoot myself.'

'Did you intend to shoot her and yourself?'

'No.'

'There were two cartridges.'

'I know.'

'One of the boys said when you brought the gun into the lounge you broke it open and looked into it. Was that when you loaded it?'

'No.'

'When your wife came downstairs you said you reasoned with her again?'

'Yes, I said: "Are you really going out?"'

'Where did she go?'

'She was in the kitchen.'

'You put the cartridges in the gun as she passed you?'

'Yes.'

'Why did you want to shoot yourself in front of her?'

'I was so miserable and wretched.'

'But why in front of her?'

'I thought it would prevent her from going out.'

'Why did you load the gun when she came into the room?'

'To shoot myself, I thought my note explains that.'

'Are you sure you did not intend to shoot your wife?'

'Not at all.'

'Is there anything in your letter which points to your death rather than your wife's?'

'Yes, there is.'

'It was quite an accident?'

'Yes.'

'You did not intend to hurt her at all?'

'No.'

These questions and Worthington's answers became the lynchpin of the court case. His defence argued that the note had been written for the police because he did not intend to be alive to tell them the details himself. In his closing statement Mr Flowers, for the defence, asked the jury to find that the victim had been shot accidentally while Worthington was attempting suicide and that they should therefore return a verdict of manslaughter. He reminded the jury that Revd Stearns had described Worthington as being devoted to his wife and how the court had heard that 'Worthington hated pain and suffering. He could not bear to see chickens killed'. Flowers said that the onus was upon the prosecution to prove that Worthington intended to kill Sybil.

The prosecution argued that if the shooting had been an accident then Worthington would have mentioned it sooner. And the same applied to his claim that he had intended suicide. Oliver, the defence counsel, felt that the letter was intended to embroil Sybil's murder in scandal and thereby drag Lionel Wright into the case with the words 'he is the cause of this tragedy'. He asked the jury to consider the statements made by Worthington's sons and ask themselves whether there had been any indication then that their father's intention had been suicide.

When Justice Hawke summed up he agreed with Flowers that the onus was on the prosecution to prove that Worthington killed her 'by a determined deliberate act'. His final words to the jury were: 'Fix in your minds this, have the prosecution proved him guilty or not?'

The jury retired for fifty-five minutes and on their return the foreman announced a guilty verdict.

The crowd outside the trial of Walter Worthington. (Author's Collection)

The judge passed the death sentence. It was Monday 20 May 1935 and the first time that this judgment had been issued since the case of Walter Horsford, the St Neots Poisoner, in 1898.

Worthington was removed to Bedford gaol. On 24 June Lord Hewart and Justices Swift and Lawrence dismissed an appeal at the Court of Criminal Appeal in London. Worthington's execution was set for 10 June at Bedford gaol. Thomas Pierrepoint hanged him at 8 a.m. on the appointed day.

The case of Walter Worthington holds no great mysteries but it seems likely that the prosecutor, Mr Oliver, hit on the truth when he asked: 'Did you intend to shoot her and yourself?' It is hard to imagine how the gun could have fired accidentally, especially when it hit Sybil with such deadly accuracy. It is equally easy to see that Worthington's state of mind was disturbed by obsessive jealousy to the extent where his plan could have included suicide.

16

OTHER NOTABLE CAMBRIDGESHIRE CRIMES

There are three other cases that are too interesting to leave out, but, in the case of this chapter, they are too sparsely documented to cover with more than a short recital. The first of these is nothing more than the contents of a handbill, which appears to be the only surviving evidence of a horrendous seventeenth-century crime. The details are vivid enough therein to offer a tantalising glimpse of the shocking events but sufficiently vague to leave the full story and final outcome as mysteries. It is worth noting that the £60 reward offered seems paltry compared to the £2,000 stolen.

The wording of the untitled handbill:

Of most notorious and barbarous, bloody and inhuman murder; committed on Sunday morning last, on the bodies of Sr Thomas Flimer Kt And Bar; his lady, one child, and five servants, near Wickham in Cambridgeshire. By 3 men and 2 woman: Particularly how they Brook into the house and kill'd the servants, and cut Sr Thomas Flimer's throat, whilest the 2 woman drove a spike through the lady's temples, and fasened her to the ground, also how they robb'd the house of the value of £2000 in moneys, besides, jewels, plate, watches, rings, and other things of great value.

Note. There is a reward of sixty pounds for any person or persons, that shall apprehend or take any of these notorious murders.

On Saturday last, Sr Thomas Flymer Kt And Bar; had invited several of their relations and friends to dine with him and his lady being it was the feasting day. And after dinner they were all very merry till about 11 or 12 o'clock at night, their relations and friends having their coaches waiting for them they broke up, and went to their dwelling houses; so about two or 3 hours after, these three notorious villains broke into the house, by having a 2 storey ladder and breaking a pane of glass in the window, one put his hand in and unhasped the casement, which the door of the room being closed and the key in it they impudently unlockt it and went directly down stairs, having a dirk lantern to light them, and let the two women in. Which they impudently enter'd, and without asking any questions went upstairs, one of 'em said, the servants was dead asleep, and I'll shew you where Sr Thomas and his lady lies, for she had been a servant in the house; so they broke open the door, which Sr Thomas hearing a noise, and seeing a light he asked who was there; with that one made answer and said we will tell you presently, and no sooner was the word out of their mouth, but he was knock down, which his lady seeing fell a screaking and crying out murder, with that one of the women stopped the lady's mouth, whilest the men cut Sr Thomas's throat. And the women they drove a spick through the lady's temples which fasted her head to the floor. Which with knocking they wakened the nurse that lay in the next room, and she hearing a noise cried out who is that, that makes such a noise to disturb my lady.

And they hearing somebody speak they were so surprised that they stood still all but she that was the maid; for she know'd her tongue so she went and broke open the door and went in, which the rest seeing followed her, then they bound and gag'd the nurse and she having a child lying by her it cried; with that she that was the maid said I'll send you out of this world presently, so took it by the heels and beat its brains out against the floor. So she knowing where the rest of the servants lay they went and murdered them; then they went and rifled the house of gold and silver to the value of £2000 besides jewels, plate, rings and other things of great value. The plate all having Sr Thomas's Coat of Arms and his name engraved at large, there was in gold a cup marked with the same and several rings, the posse (sic) of the lady's wedding ring (was Christ alone made us two in one). And in plate, 4 dishes, a dozen of plates, six poringers, 4 candlesticks, a dozen of spoons, a dozen of forks and a dozen of silver-hasted knives; all marked with aforesaid mark. And after they had done what mischief they could they packed up all and went clear with their booty between five and six, leaving the nurse bound and gag'd, not murdered, by which means it's hoped they will be found out, in order to be brought to trial and receive that justice which becomes due for such a horrid and barbarous a fact as that was. And in the morning about nine o'clock, a poor man goes to dress the horses for the coach-man, as he always did every Sunday morning, for he got a dinner for his family every Sunday; so he goes as formerly he did and rings at the gate, but nobody came to let him in, with that he goes home and tells his wife, that nobody would let him in, perhaps their being late up last night, Cries she they are not stirring, know no cries he they near lay a bed till this time a day; and he goes again and rings nobody came, and just as he was a going away he espied the marks of a bloody hand upon the post, so he goes back to the town and takes a constable and other assistance and broke open the gate, where they found Sr Thomas, his lady and their child murdered, the nurse bound and gag'd and the rest of the servants murdered as aforesaid. The house robbed, so they unbound and ungagged the nurse and she declared as aforesaid. But by this we see the temptations of Satan as great, which shall force a man for the lucre of a little worldly pels (*sic*), suffer disgrace here, and hazard the loss of his soul without repentance, and that to all eternity.

A reward of sixty pounds is offered by Sr Thomas's brother Sr Edward Flimer, living at Stratford a mile beyond Bow, to any person or persons that shall take, or cause to be taken, any of these notorious murderers. Likewise all goldsmiths, pawnbrokers, or others are desired if any of the aforesaid jewels, plate, or rings, should be offered to sale or pawn, that they would be so kind as to stop the goods and the party that offers them to sale, and their cost and charges shall be paid, besides the sixty pounds be Edward Flimer, that they may be brought to justice.

Licensed according to Order.

Not a Ghost of a Chance

Without a great deal of original documentation to work from, it seems most appropriate to present a succinct account of the Gervais Matcham story. Matcham's Gibbet was located on the road out of Alconbury opposite the entrance of what is now the company, Huntingdon Life Sciences. It can be found on some old maps at the Woolley turning of the Great North Road just north of Brampton Hut and was named after Gervais Matcham whose body was left to hang there to rot after his execution in 1786.

Six years before his execution Matcham had murdered a 15-year-old named Benjamin Jones at the same spot. His gibbet remained in place until well into the nineteenth century.

Matcham was born in Yorkshire around 1760 and ran away from home when he was 12 to fulfil his ambition of becoming a jockey. He had a talent for handling horses and he found work as a stable hand assisting the Duke of Northumberland's stable manager in the transportation of horses abroad. He also worked as, among other things, a horse dealer. Eventually he enlisted in the infantry but did not take to his new role. By 1780 he had deserted and was again loitering around the world of horses, this time at Huntingdon races.

He was struggling to find adequate food or shelter and in the end decided that the best place to hide would be back in the army. He therefore re-enlisted, this time becoming a private in the 49th Huntingdonshire Foot Regiment.

Matcham got on well with people and was liked and trusted by both his comrades and superiors, including Quartermaster Sergeant Jones. On 18 August 1780 Matcham was ordered to be chaperone to the Quartermaster's son, Benjamin, who was the regiment's 15-year-old drummer boy. Benjamin was going to walk approximately five miles to Diddington Hall to collect seven pounds from Major Reynolds. The money, all in gold coins, was to be used to buy supplies.

The journey to Diddington Hall passed without incident, but as they walked back to their regiment Matcham decided that he was going to steal the money. They reached a fork in the road and Matcham convinced his companion that they should take a wrong turning, which led them past isolated woodland. It was then that Matcham attacked, pulling a knife from under his tunic and slitting young Jones's throat.

Matcham dragged the dying drummer boy into undergrowth and covered the body with leaves and branches before fleeing the area with the money. It took some time for the body to be discovered, but by then Matcham was almost impossible to find as he had travelled north to York and been press-ganged into the Navy.

The ghost of Benjamin Jones. (George Cruikshank)

After several years Matcham was discharged from the service. One night shortly thereafter he was walking across Salisbury Plain with a comrade when a storm broke out. The story goes that they kept walking until they were suddenly confronted by the vision of an old woman. Both saw this and Matcham's companion ran away. As Matcham walked on alone he saw other apparitions until eventually he was faced with the vision of Jesus on one side of the road and Benjamin Jones on the other.

Matcham's visions were most likely to be the product of a disturbed mind, but undoubtedly he believed them to be genuine. The idea that they were real no doubt helped to make the story famous in its day. Matcham ran to the nearest town and confessed. He was transported to Huntingdon and convicted at the next assizes. As a deserter he stood trial in the uniform of the 49th Huntingdonshire Foot Regiment.

Because of his own confession he was found guilty and sentenced to death. The judge ordered that after his execution his body was to hang at the spot where he had killed his victim. Matcham's body, still dressed in his red uniform, was left to rot on its gibbet, the bones and tattered cloth remaining long after his flesh had rotted.

The tale of Benjamin Jones and Gervais Matcham was told in an extremely long poem entitled *The Dead Drummer: A Legend of Salisbury Plain*. It is part of a collection of humorous and macabre stories published in the *Ingoldsby Legends* by Thomas Ingoldsby – the pen name of Revd Richard H. Barham. These were published in three series between 1840 and 1847 with illustrations from George Cruikshank.[1]

Lost in the Brooding Fen

The final of these short case histories is an example of one for which there has been plenty of rumour and speculation but, so far at least, no conclusive solution.

Richard Peak was from Caxton, where he lived with his widowed mother and his two younger siblings. Richard was christened in 1831 and was therefore about 20 when the Cambridgeshire police force was formed in 1851. In 1852 he joined up and became a constable in December of that year. He was stationed at Burwell and given the responsibility for the village of Wicken about two miles away.

In 1854 he married a Soham girl named Ann Dennis Cooper, the daughter of Joseph Wood Cooper. Before their marriage she had lived in the house where Soham vicarage now is. After their nuptials they were given permission to live together in the police house at Burwell.

Their first child was a son named Sidney and by August 1855 they were expecting their second child. On Friday 17 August of that year Peak was ordered to police a crop auction taking place at Wicken's Lion public house. The auction was due to finish at 9 p.m. but Peak's shift was to start at 5 a.m. He reported for duty and left Burwell for the walk to Wicken wearing his police constable's uniform.

Later William Cranwell, the landlord, reported that Constable Peak had made several visits to the bar during the evening and was not wearing his uniform at the time. Drinking on duty was strictly against the rules and the landlord claimed that Peak had consumed 'a pint of beer and a shilling's worth of brandy' which may have explained why he was dressed in civilian clothes. But another explanation was that constables were often allowed to change into private clothes at night for events such as this to save their day uniforms. Whatever the reason, Peak would have needed to be back in his uniform when he was next due to see his sergeant. This meeting was scheduled for 4 a.m. back at Burwell.

During the evening plenty of people witnessed Peak in the bar and in the garden, and also breaking up a minor disturbance in the pub. People began to disperse in the early hours and at 3.15 a.m. Cranwell saw the constable for the last time. Peak was leaving and said: 'Good morning. I've got an hour and a half's walk, and then I will go to bed.'

Constable Peak failed to report to his sergeant at 4 a.m. In the following days many people were interviewed and police were drafted in from elsewhere to search routes from Wicken to Burwell. Various stories

Wicken Fen in the 1800s. (Cambridgeshire Collection, Cambridge Central Library)

A family photograph of PC Peak. It was printed on to glass, which accounts for its crazed effect. (Peterborough Police Museum)

emerged; three men had been seen fighting in Wicken; a brick kiln at Burwell Fen had been giving off 'a very peculiar and disagreeable smell'; and rumours circulated about a local gang known as The Fen Tigers, but none led to Peak.

After his disappearance his wife gave birth to their second child, named Alfred. The following year a man on his deathbed stated that Peak had been murdered by a blow to the head. He claimed he had not com-mitted the crime himself, nor would he name the man who had, but said that the body had been disposed of in the kiln. But there was nothing to substantiate the story and eventually the story died down again.

In the 1880s a skeleton was pulled from a pond in Wicken. It was seen to have suffered severe damage to the skull. Strangely the remains were returned to the pond and lost. During renovation work at the Anchor pub in Burwell a skeleton was discovered. For years the skull was displayed over the bar and it was rumoured to be PC Peak's. Eventually it was dropped and smashed and the whereabouts of the other bones are not known. Interestingly the Anchor is located on the Wicken side of Burwell, and seems to be the most probable of the three rumoured resting places of PC Peak.

The widow returned to live with her parents in Soham. She lived to the age of 80 and was buried in Soham's Fordham Road cemetery near the grave of her eldest son, Sidney. Sidney's descendants continued to live in Soham and in recent years donated the above photograph of Constable Peak to the police museum in Peterborough.

Notes
1 George Cruikshank (1792–1878) was a humorist of the Hogarth school. He produced more than 15,000 drawings in his lifetime and many consider him to be one of Britain's finest book illustrators.

SELECT BIBLIOGRAPHY

Barham, Thomas, *The Ingoldsby Legends*, Ward Lock.

Bell, John, *Cambridgeshire Crimes*, Popular Publications, St Ives, 1994.

——, *More Crimes of Cambridgeshire*, Popular Publications, St Ives, 1995.

Blackstone, William, *Commentaries on the Laws of England*, Clarendon Press, Oxford, 1765–9.

Church, Robert, *Murder in East Anglia*, Hale, London, 1987.

The Complete Newgate Calendar, Navarre Society Ltd, London, 1926.

Eddleston, John J., *The Encyclopedia of Executions*, John Blake, London, 2002.

Gibbons, Thomas, *An Account of a Most Terrible Fire*, James Buckland, London, 1769.

Gillen, Mollie, *Assassination of the Prime Minister*, Sidgwick and Jackson, London, 1972.

Hawkins, Sir Henry, *The Reminiscences of Sir Henry Hawkins (Baron Brampton)*, Thomas Nelson and Sons, London, 1909.

Narrative of the Murder of the late Rev. J. Waterhouse, T. Lovell, Huntingdon, 1827.

Oxford Dictionary of National Biography, Oxford University Press, Oxford, 1982.

Richardson, Heather, *Burwell, A Stroll Through History*, H.M. Richardson Publishing, Cambridge, 1990.

Stevens, Serita with Anne Klarner, *Deadly Doses*, F. and W. Publications, Cincinnati, 1990.

Wright, W., *A Sermon . . . occasioned by the barbarous murder of the Rev. J. Waterhouse*, A.P. Wood, Huntingdon, 1827.

Newspapers and Journals

Cambridge Advertiser

Cambridge Chronicle

Cambridge Chronicle and University Journal

Cambridge Daily News

Cambridge Evening News

Cambridge Express: and Eastern Counties Weekly News

Cambridge Independent Press

Ely Standard

Evening Standard

Gentleman's Magazine

Huntingdonshire Gazette

Hunts Post

Illustrated Police News

Isle of Ely Herald

The Leader

Norwich Mercury

Stamford Mercury

Sunday Telegraph magazine

The Times

ACKNOWLEDGEMENTS

Jacen, Natalie, Lana and Dean for making home a lovely place to work.

Bob Burn-Murdoch at the Norris Museum, St Ives, David Bushby, Stewart and Rosie Evans, Chris Jakes at the Cambridgeshire Collection, Laura Johnston at the *Cambridge Evening News*, Donal O'Danachair at www.exclassics.com, Mike Petty, David Rudd at the St Neots Museum and Jonathon Smith at Trinity College Library for their help with research and illustrations.

Maureen Algar, Christine Bartram, Mark Billingham, Sarah Bryce, Barry Crowther, Broo Doherty, Alison Hilborne, Kimberley Jackson-Liew, Sheila Malham, Jennifer Marrs, Richard Reynolds, Floramay Waterhouse and Kate Wyatt for their advice and encouragement.